D ebra Kandelaars brings over fifteen years' experience in television production and writing to the difficult task of compiling 'a few favourites' from the twelve hundred or so *Postcards* stories written over the last seven years. Debra has an MA in Creative Writing and works as a freelance writer and editor on a variety of projects including websites and creative business documents. Debra lives in Adelaide with *Postcards*' producer, Ron Kandelaars, their children and a variety of animals.

Postcards
A few of our favourites

Compiled and edited by Debra Kandelaars

Written by Debra Kandelaars, Ron Kandelaars, Keith Conlon

and Mike Sexton from original television scripts

Wakefield Press

Above: Grenfell Street, Adelaide   **Photo by Mick Bradley**

Wakefield Press
17 Rundle Street
Kent Town
South Australia 5067

First published 2001
Reprinted 2002

Copyright ©
Channel 9 South Australia
Pty Ltd, Adelaide, 2001

Designed by Dean Lahn,
Lahn Stafford Design
Typeset by Clinton Ellicott,
Wakefield Press
Printed and bound by
Hyde Park Press

National Library of Australia
Cataloguing-in-publication
entry

Postcards: A few of
our favourites.

ISBN 1 86254 560 X.

1. Postcards (Television
program). 2. South
Australia – Guidebooks.
I. Conlon, Keith. II. Sexton,
Mike. III. Kandelaars, Debra.
IV. Kandelaars, Ron.

Contents

Introduction

by Keith Conlon

Q How do you keep Postcards' team members quiet?
A Ask them for their favourite place in South Australia.

It works every time. They glaze over as their 'video-of-the-mind' searches through hundreds of images from hot ochres to cool greens and hosts of experiences from the exhilarating to the enchanting.

As one of the founding group back in October 1995, I'm in more trouble than most, with a long list of destinations where I want to spend time with my family. They start round the corner and end at the faraway border of our vast mosaic of a state.

Let us admit, then, that this is not our definitive list of favourites – these are only some of them. What's more, each time we venture out to meet a park ranger, say, or portray a hidden pocket, invariably we encounter another story along the way.

Meanwhile, in city and rural corners, enthusiastic and interesting characters are opening up new places to stay and savour their surrounds, or using everything from clay to red-gum to evoke their deep sense of belonging to this land. We're particularly grateful to those new and old South Australian interpreters who produce new trails, tours, signs, guidebooks and histories that reveal the intricacies of our environment and heritage. Some of our mosaic is muted and subtle. South Australia is not for the flashy, wham-bam 'Wallyworld' tourist, rather it's a vast tapestry of many colours and moods. Its beauty and significance often emerge more sharply as we learn from our invaluable local guides.

That's why we don't think of *Postcards* as a tourism or travel program. Surely it has become a valuable resource for planning everything from a Sunday drive to a caravan crawl for as long as it takes. But we trust you find it is more than that. We hope you enjoy the stories as windows into the soul of this region . . . as we ask why it's like it is and how things happened.

Some of Australia's best heritage towns serve as illustrations. Robe is a beautifully restored, mid-nineteenth-century colonial port town because the advent of south-east rail lines left it stranded and safe from 'progress'. Morgan, on the other hand, is the fruit of a new railway, a living museum of a river-port town that emerged within months of a line linking the Big Bend on the Murray with the city, only to be left out of the main-stream as even more railways killed the mighty paddle steamer era. Burra, meanwhile, slipped from its status as the biggest inland town in the continent over one-and-a-half centuries back while the Monster Mine was at its peak, to become a richly endowed pastoral centre just inside the badlands. Another few kilometres eastward and it would have become a desert ghost town.

On a personal note, the themes and stories that I enjoy most are the ones you won't read in the travel brochures. They emerge as I learn more about our past and present and I know the team feels similarly. Somehow we are the lucky ones who are asked to

apply our craft to a task that's at once a privilege and a lot fun along the way. (The crew tips are included so that you can avoid some of our silliest predicaments.)

Now, at last, some of our twelve-hundred or more stories so far have made it into this print edition. They give us a chance to relive great moments round the corner and round the vastness of our state. As they expose the joys on our doorstep, we hope they pass one of our basic tests and have you saying 'I didn't know that!' And that they get you out there soon.

Editor's Note

My thanks to Ron Kandelaars, Keith Conlon, Jeff Clayfield, Trevor Griscti, Andrew McEvoy, Lisa McAskill and former producer Mike Sexton for their photos and ideas, and to the students from the Flinders University Cultural Tourism course who helped with research on selected stories. Special thanks to Bernd Stoecker and Pete Dobre for generously providing photographs from their superb portfolios; to the Royal Automobile Association (SA) for supplying such useful maps; to Gina Inverarity and Michael Bollen from Wakefield Press for their warmth, cooperation and efficiency in helping to turn our idea into reality; Dean Lahn and Clinton Ellicott for fabulous design and typesetting; and my sister, Jenni Crawley, for all her help on the home front. Thanks also to my husband Ron for his boundless love and faith in me, to my parents Judy and Barry Grosse for their love and encouragement, and my children Alexandra and Grace for their youthful sparkle. The *Postcards* website is created by World Wide Web Architects.

Debra Kandelaars

Meet the Postcards Team

Channel Nine's *Postcards* program came to life in Adelaide in 1995 with the aim of showcasing South Australia's remarkable places and characters. Since then, *Postcards* has collected three South Australian Tourism Awards, and the program now graces the South Australian Tourism Hall of Fame.

Every Sunday evening, hundreds of thousands of South Australians tune in at five-thirty to watch the team present a myriad of stories from all over the state. But there's always more to a yarn than what you see. Behind the scenes, *Postcards* team-members work just as enthusiastically – recording, researching, writing and editing – to ensure the program gets to air every week. So, meet the team . . .

From left: Mark Bickley, Ron Kandelaars, Lisa McAskill, Michael Keelan, Keith Conlon

Keith Conlon, Host/Writer Keith Conlon brings over thirty years experience as a broadcast journalist and storyteller to the enviable task of identifying, recording and writing about each episode's host location. He has a passion for all things South Australian and his knowledge about our state is encyclopaedic, hence his honorary name 'Mr South Australia'. Keith has hosted *Postcards* since it first began in 1995 and is one of the state's best-known media personalities.

Ron Kandelaars, Producer/Writer For Ron Kandelaars, the 'dream' job of *Postcards* producer, writer and reporter allows him to combine a few of his passions: South Australia, outdoor adventures and storytelling. Ron has over twenty years' experience as a television journalist and public relations consultant. He says the role of producer is 'a fantastic opportunity that gives me the scope to scour the state for stories and provide viewers with a greater insight into what they can find in South Australia'.

Lisa McAskill, Presenter Lisa McAskill's extensive media experience in modelling, television and film, along with her easy-going style combine to lend a distinctly approachable and professional quality to *Postcards*. During her career she has appeared in numerous television commercials along with presenting a range of programs and corporate events. Lisa is South Australian born and bred and is passionate about high-lighting all the fabulous places and people she encounters on her travels as one of the *Postcards* team.

Mark Bickley, Guest Presenter Former captain of the Adelaide Crows football team, Mark Bickley recently turned his hand to television and he likes what he sees. As a guest presenter on the program, Mark initially shared his home town, Port Pirie, with *Postcards* viewers. Since then, Mark has made regular guest appearances on the program bringing his own laid-back style to a range of stories. (Much to the team's delight, he even had a kick of footy with them at Football Park.)

Michael Keelan, Guest Presenter Michael Keelan is South Australia's gardening guru. With over 25 years' experience in the gardening business, his expertise extends to commercial and public building projects, gardening shows, exhibitions and radio and television presentations. Michael brings his backyard wisdom to *Postcards* as he reveals the many unique and remarkable gardens found in our state.

Jeff Clayfield, Cameraman Jeff Clayfield's photography has graced the *Postcards* screen since 1995. Jeff's long and varied career at Channel Nine has provided him with the opportunity to work on major sporting events including the Australian Grand Prix and World Series Cricket along with regular camera work for National Nine News. Jeff loves travel, photography, boating and fishing. He says, '*Postcards* has given me the chance to combine all my interests through its wide variety of stories and locations. For me, it's certainly a dream job.'

From left: Andrew McEvoy, Keith Conlon, Ron Kandelaars, Jeff Clayfield, Trevor Griscti (kneeling)

Trevor Griscti, Audio Operator Trevor Griscti studied sound for three years before starting as a videotape operator for Channel Nine in 1984. Six years later, Trevor landed the position of audio operator and began working on major sporting events including World Series Cricket, international soccer matches and the Australian Grand Prix. Trevor has recorded sound for *Postcards* since 1999. He loves spending time off with his family and says, 'The best thing about working on *Postcards* is discovering new places in South Australia that I can take them back to visit.'

Andrew McEvoy, Cameraman Andrew is a keen photographer whose work (including shots he's taken on the road with the *Postcards* team) has featured in exhibitions and as part of the Adelaide Festival Fringe. Andrew worked in public radio, and as a volunteer firefighter, before starting at Channel Nine in 1993. Since then he's worked as a sound recordist, a studio cameraman and as a field cameraman for National Nine News and *Postcards*. Andrew says, 'It's a special experience visiting the places and filming the stories of the state. It's a rewarding job all the way through to seeing the story go to air.'

Marc Orrock, Videotape Editor Marc Orrock has shaped camera tapes into *Postcards* stories since 1998. Marc began his career as a camera operator at Port Pirie Central TV in 1990 before landing the job of editor with National Nine News. Marc has a passion for music and says, 'I love matching good music with pictures to draw an emotional response from our audiences.' Marc studies movies and television programs for ideas and says editing *Postcards* has inspired him to visit many of the locations featured on the program.

Brenton Harris, Videotape Editor Brenton Harris brings 27 years of editing experience to *Postcards*. Every week he edits Keith Conlon's host pieces, collects the edited stories and pulls the program together. Brenton has edited *Postcards* since 1998 and has a background in news and current affairs, documentaries, sport and children's television. Brenton's main interests are his family and computers and he says, 'I'm a typical arm-chair viewer. The best thing about watching *Postcards* is that it's interesting to find out about where I live.'

Postcards would also like to thank the many NWS Channel Nine staff not mentioned here who have contributed to the program's success.

Adelaide

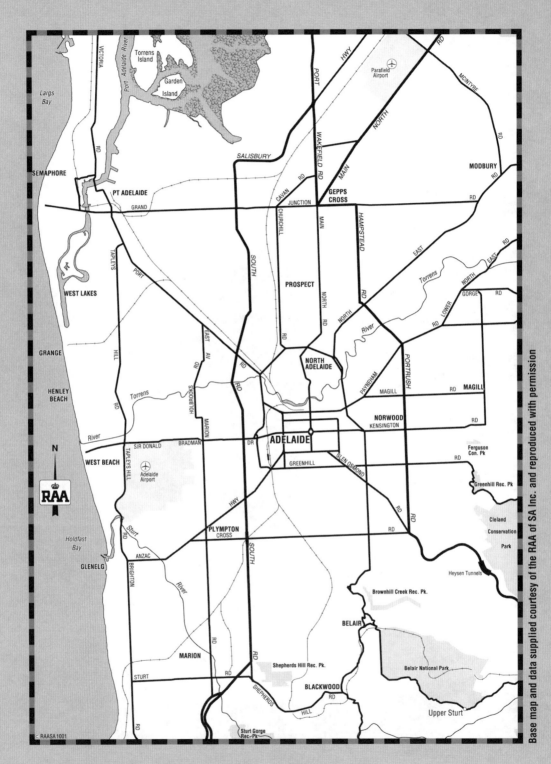

Reverse: Adelaide, a city in a park   Photo by Mick Bradley

Adelaide is a friendly, lively city renowned for its world-class food and wine, innovative cultural festivals, architectural heritage and wondrous sense of space.

A delaide was designed by Colonel William Light in 1837 as a city of one square mile, bordered by parklands. Today, the city has one million residents sprawled along a coastline stretching north and south along Gulf St Vincent, and the Adelaide Hills to the east. Adelaide is a friendly, lively city renowned for its world-class food and wine, innovative cultural festivals, architectural heritage and wondrous sense of space.

The Kaurna were the traditional Aboriginal occupants of the Adelaide area and European settlement had a devastating effect on their way of life. Clans were dispossessed of their lands and attempts by colonists to 'civilise' the Kaurna resulted in the breakdown of traditional customs and beliefs, which in turn led to reliance on charity, and in many cases, disease and death. Kaurna people still live in Adelaide today, and visitors can experience elements of their culture, both contemporary and historic, at Tandanya Aboriginal Cultural Institute and the Australian Aboriginal Cultures Gallery at the South Australian Museum.

The romantic statue of Colonel William Light on Montiefiore Hill, North Adelaide, symbolises the surveyor-general's hopes and dreams for the new city of Adelaide. Beneath the romance, however, lies the story of a man whose mission involved constant battles with ailing health and inadequate resources. By all accounts, Light was hard-working, thorough, and passionate about his plans for the colony, but he had political enemies constantly undermining his efforts. In 1839, three years after the colony was

Tips From the Crew

- Lisa suggests Lucia's in the Central Market for fantastic coffee and authentic Italian pizzas. While you're at the Market head across Gouger Street to Wilson's Organics for delicious organic wine, meat, fruit and vegetables, and pasta.

- Ron says the Hill Billy Hoot on the balcony of 3D Radio at Stepney is great fun. Guitarists and singers join in to play wonderful renditions of country classics. It's on every Monday night and is broadcast on 93.7 FM from 8 to 9 pm.

- Jeff suggests a visit to the beautifully ornate Shri Ganesha Hindu Temple at Oaklands Park. It's open to the public from 11 am to 1 pm daily, and evenings except Sunday.

- Trevor highly recommends the chilli quail at the Vietnam Restaurant at Pennington.

- Keith puts the parklands high on the family action list, especially an espresso and a rowing-boat excursion to Rymill Park and a bike ride around the Torrens Weir and Bonython Park tracks.

established, Light's health gave way, and this 'illegitimate son of an illegitimate son' died leaving debts of over six hundred pounds. Hundreds attended his funeral at Holy Trinity Church on North Terrace and he was buried in Light Square bearing a breast-plate inscribed 'Founder of Adelaide'.

At the time of Light's death Adelaide was a shanty town of tents and makeshift housing, and the immigrants who disembarked at Port Misery (Port River) were confronted with mud, marshes, mosquitoes and disappointment, having already endured uncomfortable ocean voyages to the new colony. Of course, our beautiful city today is quite different to all this, although many would argue that ruthless politics and the odd tent city still exist here!

... boats pull into the wharf and sell fresh fish to those who can get out of bed early enough on a Sunday morning.

Port Adelaide fish market   Photo by Milton Wordley

Adelaide's original European residents began their journey into the colony near today's Port Adelaide. After many years of dilapidation, this area has recently been injected with new life and energy. Old buildings and warehouses have been converted into apartments, there are great pubs and restaurants, a weekend market, an excellent Maritime Museum and lots

I Didn't Know That!

- Before Colonel William Light's death in 1839, he was so poor he was forced to sell sketches for a living.

- The legendary bite-size pies and pasties at Perryman's Bakery in North Adelaide were first designed during the Depression to make them affordable.

- An Adelaide newspaper reported in 1860 that 'the healthful and invigorating exercise of football is becoming popular here'.

- The Adelaide Parklands cover around 720 hectares and make up almost half of the city area.

- Before stately Government House was built, Governor Hindmarsh's vice regal residence was a damp, three-roomed, mud-walled house built by sailors.

- In the late 1800s, there was a rollercoaster and a cycling track at Adelaide Oval.

of interesting people. Around on the North Arm, boats pull into the wharf and sell fresh fish to those who can get out of bed early enough on a Sunday morning. Nearby Semaphore is reminiscent of an old-fashioned seaside town with a wide main street dotted with cafes and antique shops.

To the south is seaside Glenelg, where South Australia was proclaimed a province by Governor Hindmarsh on 28 December 1836. Glenelg was named after the colonial secretary, who reportedly perfected the art of doing nothing. It fits well then, that today it is a fun destination for shopping, food and relaxation.

Further south, Adelaide's flat coastline begins to rise into majestic cliffs at Seacliff and Marino Rocks. Nearby, you can join the Tjilbruke trail, based on a Kaurna 'songline' that tells the story of springs created by Tjilbruke's tears as he wept for his murdered nephew. The trail winds down the Fleurieu Peninsula from Kingston Park to Cape Jervis.

It's about half an hour's drive from Adelaide's coastline to the Mount Lofty Ranges. In the foothills, you'll find stunning conservation parks such as Morialta, with ancient cliffs, thick scrub and waterfalls in winter. You can go for a wander and dabble in rock pools, then finish with coffee and scones at Waterfall Gully or try cycling the scenic Torrens Linear Park that meanders from the foothills to the sea.

... tip-toe along balconies and touch precious artefacts on the 'White Gloves' tour ...

North Terrace is almost always listed as the tourist's starting point to the city itself. So off we go. Gaze at the Art Gallery of South Australia's wondrous works, wander around Adelaide University's historic campus and down to the River Torrens (where Adelaide's early settlers camped), gather in the beautifully restored Jervois Wing for a White Gloves tour of the Mortlock Library's South Australiana treasures, score some information about our legendary cricketer at the Bradman Museum, picnic under the giant Moreton Bay Fig trees in Botanic Park, check out the newly revamped, coloured-glass Palm House at the

Palm House, Botanic Gardens

Botanic Gardens, enter the world of the Freemasons on a tour of the Masonic Lodge, peek over the huge stone wall of Government House (or wait for an open day), have a coffee in Rundle Street, spend your money in the Mall, cruise the bookshops in Hindley Street, watch the Sunday morning petanque players in the East End, eat fantastic food at dozens of restaurants, stand on the Festival Centre balcony and take in the view of Elder Park and the river, have lunch at Jolley's Boathouse and watch the paddleboats go by, get on a paddleboat or the *Popeye* passenger boat and glide around Torrens Lake. And when you've had enough, head over to Rundle, Gouger or Hutt street for culinary joy.

Adelaide is famous for its Central Market and rightly so. Surrounded by Gouger Street and Chinatown restaurants, it's a noisy, colourful, crowded place where you can buy absolutely anything that's edible. Exotic fruits and vegetables, herbs, fresh pasta, olive oil, wine, coffee, cheeses, fish, hot cashews, fantastic German cured meats and sausages, exquisite cakes and pastries . . . yum!

Adelaide's architecture is a grand legacy of British colonisation: beautiful churches and cathedrals, magnificent stone homes, and regal city buildings, all monuments to a handcrafted era. Former villages like Mitcham, Unley, Henley Beach and Norwood now blend into the suburbs, but each has its own character and most have retained a village feel with al fresco restaurants, cafes, pubs, cinemas and shops at their beating heart.

And best of all, it's easy to get around here. Adelaide has all the benefits of a large, multicultural city without the congestion – and most of her charms are a short drive or walk from the city centre. Add to this an accommodating Mediterranean climate, and you have the perfect blend to explore everything Adelaide has to offer.

Want More Information?

SA Visitor and Travel Centre
1300 655 276

Port Adelaide Visitor Centre
(08) 8447 4788

Glenelg Visitor Centre
(08) 8294 5833

Adelaide Passenger Transport
(08) 8210 1000

National Parks and Wildlife SA
(08) 8204 1910

RAA Touring (maps and guides)
(08) 8205 4540

SA Tourism Commission website
www.southaustralia.com

***Postcards* website**
www.postcards.sa.com.au

Penfold's Magill Estate
with Keith Conlon

It's in Adelaide's suburban back yard, and it's increasingly a mecca for international winelovers. Dr Penfold's original plantings seven kilometres from the colonial capital were for medical purposes, but they grew into the winery that would produce Australia's flagship wine: Penfold's Grange.

The 1955 vintage of the Grange was recently included in the prestigious American Wine Spectator's 'Dozen of the Century'. As the magazine puts it, '... the Grange ushered in a new era in Australian winemaking'.

The seeds of the revolution were planted with the arrival of Dr Christopher Penfold, his wife, Mary, and daughter Georgina in the fledging colony of South Australia in 1844. They bought a farm at Magill, and were soon making port wine for their anaemic patients from their imported cuttings. They built a cottage and named it after Mary's home in Surrey – The Grange. Visitors to the restored Magill winery can now join a 'Great Grange Tour' that takes them into the original drawing room, before sampling the wine that took its name from a humble cottage. A remaining pocket of the original vines now provides the vintage for Penfold's Magill Estate Shiraz. It's made using the same techniques and tanks that produced one of the great wines of the world.

In the historic vintage cellars there are rows of wax-lined square concrete tanks that were the domain of Max Schubert, Penfold's chief winemaker. Max was sent to Europe in 1948, where he fell in love with the great long-living reds of Bordeaux. He dared to think he might make such a wine in Australia, and he did! At the time, 90 per cent of the nation's output was sherry and port. Max's Grange was the wine that

A complete, priceless collection of the Grange rests in Max Schubert's Grotto at Penfold's Magill Estate

literally changed the landscape, particularly in South Australia, where new mass plantings for export wine still roll across its wine regions.

Deep in the tunnels cut under the hillside is a grotto that serves as a shrine to the Grange and its creator. Here the experimental vintages are matured in quick, dark, cool cellars crowded with small American oak barrels. At the end of one tunnel rests a complete, priceless collection of the Grange. Max Schubert gave away most of the first small batch of Grange in 1951. At the last auction sale, a bottle brought over forty-five-thousand dollars. An official company tasting of the first few years' vintage was, in Max's words, 'absolutely disastrous. No one liked it'. He was told, in writing, to stop. But Max persisted, and he secretly made three more vintages.

When the 1955 had matured, it won gold in the Sydney wine show and Max, who was the office boy for Penfold's Nuriootpa winery at the time, was asked to start making the Grange again. He was transferred to Magill and, with a swag of night-school chemistry lessons to add to his natural talents, he graduated to chief winemaker. In 1971, the Grange took top honours at the Paris Wine Olympiad.

For its 150th anniversary, Penfolds gave the historic Magill winery a ten-million-dollar treat. Max's Grange grotto was laid out and lit for hourly tours, and the old potstill building now sits as a tasting room and cellar door for the family of reds and whites that are behind the Grange. There's also a striking minimalist architecture restaurant offering Grange by the glass, fine cuisine and stunning city views.

You can visit the Penfold's Magill Estate vineyard daily for tours and tastings.

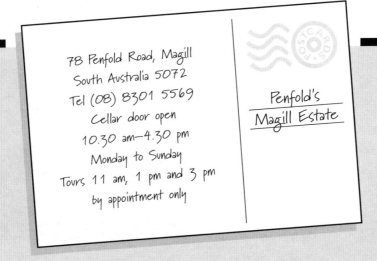

78 Penfold Road, Magill
South Australia 5072
Tel (08) 8301 5569
Cellar door open
10.30 am—4.30 pm
Monday to Sunday
Tours 11 am, 1 pm and 3 pm
by appointment only

Penfold's
Magill Estate

Adelaide Oval Tour

with Mark Bickley

First stop on the Adelaide Oval heritage tour is the Bradman Stand where you get a bird's-eye view of one of the most picturesque sporting grounds in the world.

There are many stories attached to this historic ground – like the roller-coaster that was a permanent fixture in the southern end until the late 1880s, and the steeply cambered cycling track that circled the oval until it was replaced by seating in 1901. Over recent years, the new lighting towers have attracted their fair share of controversy, although it seems there were similar plans in the 1880s, when the first night match of local football was played.

For me, the journey into the change rooms under the Sir Edwin Smith Stand represents a trip back in time:

Adelaide Oval was carved out of the parklands in 1871

'I played my first SANFL game here with South Adelaide more than a decade ago and as a twenty-year-old the honour board always instilled a great sense of tradition – footy has been played here for well over a century.'

The last Grand Final was played at the oval in 1973 between North Adelaide and Glenelg. Over the years, Adelaide Oval has seen some momentous tussles, but its international reputation stems from well over a century of first-class cricket, with some of the great Test matches of all time played here.

The Adelaide Oval tour takes you into the players' world, where many a nervous cricketer has watched the action below. But surely one of the most interesting tales dates back to what is now known as the Bodyline series between Australia and the old enemy, England. One particular day's play drew a record crowd of fifty thousand and the crowd favourite, the legendary Don Bradman, was cut to normal size by the unpopular bodyline tactic. England began to dominate, tempers flared and officials went to extraordinary lengths to protect the pitch. The ground's nightwatchman was armed with a gun to stave off potential saboteurs. Fortunately, nobody turned up to test him.

The photos in the committee room take you through the amazing history of a ground carved out of the parklands back in 1871. The first Test played here was between Australia and England in 1884. In the early days, many spectators didn't pay as they watched the action from above at Montefiore Hill, but soon the Moreton Bay fig trees dominated the skyline and put an end to that.

The scoreboard operators would have witnessed some great play over the years and visitors who join the tour today can experience this piece of Adelaide's heritage first-hand. Built in 1911 for just £1500, the scoreboard is still operated by bicycle chains and rotating numbers, keeping watchful spectators up to date in the good old-fashioned way.

It's just part of the Adelaide Oval Tour which runs each Tuesday and Thursday. And while you're in this neck of the woods, why not take a quick stroll up to North Terrace for another 'hit' of legendary sporting history at the Bradman Collection.

Adelaide Oval, North Adelaide
South Australia 5006
Tel (08) 8300 3800
Tuesday and Thursday at 10 am.
Meet at the
Phil Ridings entrance, southern end

Adelaide
Oval Tour

The Bradman Collection
with Mark Bickley

The outpouring of public emotion following the death of Sir Donald Bradman was yet more proof that 'The Don' remains Australia's greatest sporting hero. Since his death, the State Library has dropped its admission charge to the Bradman Collection, ensuring that many more sports lovers will come to understand the achievements of a man whose feats on the cricket field galvanised a young country and gave it heart during the black days of the Great Depression.

The bat from one of his greatest Test innings, 334 against the old enemy England at Headingley in Leeds in 1930, takes pride of place in the collection. For many years it remained a Test match record and while it has now been bettered by the likes of West Indians Brian Lara and Sir Garfield Sobers, and equalled by former Australian Captain Mark Taylor, 334 remains a benchmark in cricket.

The Collection's in-house video gives a fascinating insight into Sir Donald's many achievements. Guide Alex Mericka has devoted much of his life to researching the feats of Sir Donald Bradman and while 'The Don's' Test average of 99.94 speaks for itself, it's the lesser-known stories that Alex has uncovered that make one of his tours so intriguing:

'A lot of people ask me about Sir Donald's fastest century. He made it up at Black Heath in the Blue Mountains in 1930 in a game between a Blue Mountains composite side and a Nepean composite side. He hit one hundred runs in three eight-ball overs.'

But no man is infallible and in 1932 the English hatched a plot later called Bodyline to stop this run machine. The Adelaide Test in 1933 saw tensions boil over. Mounted troopers were called in to assist the police, and on one occasion there were 147 troopers with bayonets at the ready in case the crowd jumped the fence.

Sir Donald Bradman established a special relationship with the State Library, making this one of the great collections in the cricketing world. Sir Donald was a great hoarder and over the years he donated many of his precious scrapbooks to the library. You can still see those as part of the White Gloves Tour, but now many of the images have been digitised for all South Australians to enjoy. You can flick through a great man's life story, dating back to his earliest sporting achievements when he first burst onto the cricketing scene. The legend lives on at the Bradman Collection in the State Library.

'The Don' remains Australia's greatest sporting hero

State Library of South Australia
Cnr North Tce
and Kintore Ave, Adelaide
South Australia 5000
Tel (08) 8207 7595
Admission is free.
Specialised guided tours
by appointment.

The Bradman
Collection

Divett Street, Port Adelaide

with Keith Conlon

For visitors from near and far, Port Adelaide is at the top of the tide for heritage and colour. And there are plenty of both in just one stretch – Divett Street, in the heart of the historic precinct. It even boasts a couple of ghosts.

Divett Street is easy to find. It's opposite a famous portside line-up, starting with an elaborate red-brick and stone police station-turned-Visitor Centre on Commercial Road, with the Courthouse and substantial Customs House reaching towards the reconstructed Port Lighthouse. Opposite that array, Divett Street begins with its own long-standing two-storey pub on the corner. The original burned down in the 1850s, and in the following year the high tide flooded through here. Divett Street is consequently higher now, backfilled with bottom-of-the-harbour dredgings.

This narrow thoroughfare was once a bustle of sights, noises and smells created by commercial traders, bankers and agents. There's still the odd shipping-agent sign and pleasure-cruise office to show the strip's continual link with a maritime past, but these days most of the buildings are home to a bunch of residents with a sense of history. Some of them are so keen about it that they volunteer as walking tour guides to tell a yarn or two.

The nearby Port Adelaide inner-shipping basin is a tranquil pond in this new century, but 120 years ago it was hectic. It was a conduit for everything, and everyone, coming and going in South Australia. A Divett Street crawl soon brings you to a grand quartet from those times, with architecture as diverse as their original portside purposes. A handsome two-storey shop previously served a timber merchant and jeweller and more recently it was an antique shop. A detailed glazed-brick building reveals its early twentieth-century origins and tells its own tale on etched-window signs. The Melbourne Steamship Company booked freight and passengers here until about forty years ago when the age of flying took off.

Divett Street was once a bustle of sights, noises and smells created by commercial traders, bankers and agents   Photo by Trevor Fox

Still serving the seagoing side with shipping agency tenants, the old National Bank has impeccable breeding. Its high renaissance revival features are probably the work of Adelaide's answer to Christopher Wren, architect Edmund Wright, who helped bring us the Adelaide Town Hall, the General Post Office and Parliament House, as well as the old city bank building that now bears his name. To complete the quartet, there's the 120-year-old gothic Divett Chambers. It once boasted a newfangled telephone connection to the city, and the *Advertiser*'s port reporters dictated the news from within. It's now been transformed into two contemporary apartments.

In Port Adelaide's heyday, Divett Street's bond stores and warehouses created horse-and-cart traffic aplenty. From the historic intersection with Lipson Street, you can sometimes admire visiting ships docked just a block away. On one corner, a fine building has stood for 125 years; its six-paned windows with fanlights provided a view for the long-gone staff of Port Adelaide Providers Pty Ltd to the Bank of Australasia on another corner. The bank's Doric columns and high parapets first welcomed seafarers and stevedores in 1891. On the third corner, in a modest single-storey building, there was once another newspaper office for the defunct *South Australian Register*. It's now work and home for antique dealers.

However it's the bond store on the fourth corner that really holds sway. Take a slight detour into the Maritime Museum – a substantial jewel of the Port – and admire the historic two-storey bluestone building too. It went up in the 1850s for a 'big wheel' of the time, Alexander Elder, a shipping agent, investor and founder of a great pastoral firm. The building was a bond store almost until its transformation into the Museum in the state's Jubilee 150 year, 1986.

If you come on a volunteer-guided walk down Divett Street, be sure to ask about the ghosts. There is one story about heavy footsteps in what is now the Gaff Gallery, but potter Peter Johnson says they haven't invaded his ceramics studio ... yet. We eavesdropped on some Divett Street residents as they took a group of visitors for an informative stroll: 'It was like a black fluid motion ... in the shape of a big cat.' These Divett Street residents should know; they live in the old warehouse concerned. Is it the ghost of a circus panther, put down by a vet who once practised in here? Next stop was across the road to the Marine Engineers Building, with its own tale of things that go bump in the night:

'At 10.30 at night, there's often a thud. The next-door neighbour and others have heard it. And one visitor has seen a 1900s-dressed lady walk up the central stairs. Did she fall? Or jump?'

Divett Street is an entertaining and historic walk, especially with the help of volunteer guides based at the excellent Port Adelaide Visitor Centre. Get out and join them in their fascinating precinct and soak up the ambience of Divett Street.

Contact Port Adelaide
Visitor Information Centre
66 Commercial Road
Port Adelaide
South Australia 5015
Tel (08) 8447 4788
Open seven days 9 am–5 pm

Divett Street
(part of
Port Walks)

Vari's Grocery, Norwood

with Ron Kandelaars

While Roberto Piatanese slices away at the footwear in his shoe repair shop, next-door-neighbour and friend, Frank Vari, is doing the same to his prosciutto. When you walk into Vari's, you enter one of Norwood's gems and a little piece of Soriano, the village in Calabria where Frank was born.

Frank Vari came to Adelaide as a young man in 1955, leaving behind his mother Stella, but taking with him his mother's love of fine food and pasta, and the secrets gathered over generations. He took over the Norwood Parade store in 1960. By then Frank had married his sweetheart, Grace, and together they slowly carved out a reputation for fine continental food that has lasted more than forty years.

Frank started his business the hard way, walking the pavements of nearby suburbs, taking down orders and, later, making his deliveries in a Morris panel van:

Frank and Grace Vari have carved out a reputation for fine continental food   Photo by Jeff Clayfield

'I used to get the order on the Monday morning and, after my round, come back here and do the order and deliver next day. Portrush Road, Payneham, St Peters and back to the shop.'

On his travels around the back streets of Norwood and beyond, Frank made many contacts and spotted plenty of olive trees, and soon produce from nearby back yards was being delivered to the shop for pickling in Frank's secret marinade. Don't bother asking for the recipe though:

'A lot of customers, they come in and ask. If I tell you and you tell them, it will be the end of my business. Don't you reckon? That's what I'm thinking.'

That secrecy extends to Vari's special coffee blend and when you see Frank at work with a big, sharp cheese knife, you soon figure a secret should remain a secret. But you feel lucky to be able to share in the contributions that Italian immigrants have made to Australian eating – like the exquisite cakes and biscuits, the lemon taralli and almond flake. While Grace Vari started off making them herself (with a little bit of help from Mum) she eventually rallied a group of local women, from a variety of Italian regions, to make a wonderful range of biscuits.

These days Frank no longer has to deliver Vari's wares. Locals beat a path to his door and many of them have been coming here for decades.

It's a long way, in time and distance, from Frank Vari's days with his mother back in Soriano, Calabria, but when you venture into Vari's Generi Alimentari Italiani you soon get a sense of the rich heritage that Frank and Grace have brought to Adelaide.

210b The Parade, Norwood
South Australia 5067
Tel (08) 8431 1682
Open Monday–Wednesday,
Friday 8 am–6 pm,
Thursday 8 am–9 pm,
Saturday 8 am–5 pm.
Closed Sunday

Vari's
Grocery

Aboriginal Cultures Gallery
with Keith Conlon

Its ornate East Wing has adorned North Terrace in Adelaide for nearly a century, and recently the South Australian Museum, a grand old lady of the boulevard, has had a twenty million dollar facelift. The Museum reopened in March 2000 with a new entrance through a modern glass-walled addition, and a new cafe and museum shop featuring views onto North Terrace. In addition, the landmark Egyptian temple column, carved on the Nile about three thousands years ago, was moved inside.

But three thousand years sounds young, compared with one of the oldest living cultures in the world. Through the Museum's new entrance, into what used to be the basement storage area, is the beginning of a journey into the Australian Aboriginal Cultures Gallery. Franchesca Cubillo is one of the curators, and she took me through the section devoted to the first of eight regional areas, the Adelaide Plains, home of the Kaurna people.

European contact saw the loss of the Kaurna people's traditional lifestyle long before the Museum's existence, so there is only a small collection of Kaurna artefacts on display. A 1920s archaeological dig in the Moana sandhills, however, revealed rich food sources. So you'll find beautifully presented shells and bones of seabirds, dingoes and long-lost bandicoots and bettongs. A compelling photograph of a senior Kaurna woman, Ivaritji, sits above the rare wallaby-skin cloak she is wrapped in. This portrait, which is also the public face of the gallery, was taken in 1928 by Museum curators after Ivaritji spent many years helping them to understand traditional Kaurna life.

There are eight regions along with many themes to explore in this beautifully presented new gallery. From interviews with contemporary Kakadu people playing on a digital screen to a wall of meticulously hand-woven fibre baskets, sourced from Arnhem Land down to the Lower Murray.

Opposite: South Australian Museum   Photo by Keith Conlon

The emphasis is 'hands-on'. Following a menu on a digital screen, I came across literally thousands of images, videos, archival film and interviews. I discovered that *pitjuri* is a natural narcotic plant with strappy leaves and tiny flowers. A map indicated it was traded from Birdsville to the Flinders Ranges. The highlight of my on-screen search, though, was a 'meeting' with 80-year-old Linda Crombie, who told a story about gathering *pitjuri* as a young girl with her grandparents.

Ivaritji, 1928

The infectious sounds of children's laughter lured me to the play-theme end of the new gallery. A superb array of painted shields line the walls. Nearby, you can watch precious archival film showing Aboriginal kids and their traditional games and toys. An early colour sequence shot on Australia's northern coast from about fifty years ago shows boys in canoes learning to beach their craft amid much mirth, while their younger brothers play with 'toy' versions. Now, in the hands-on section, you can hold one yourself – adult and guided school groups are allowed into the play box! There are improvised balls and fine-coiled reed baskets, but the winner is definitely the 'trucka-trucka', a painted food tin with gravel inside to make it nice and noisy, and fencing wire handles for wheeling it around.

It's impossible to absorb all of the riches of this wonderful collection, spread over two levels of the Museum, in one visit. Be prepared for a return trip! The Museum's website lets you sample its enormous digitised artefacts and media collection before you head in there.

North Terrace, Adelaide
South Australia 5000
Tel (08) 207 7500
website www.samuseum.sa.gov.au
Open every day 10 am to 5 pm.
Free admission

Aboriginal
Cultures
Gallery,
SA Museum

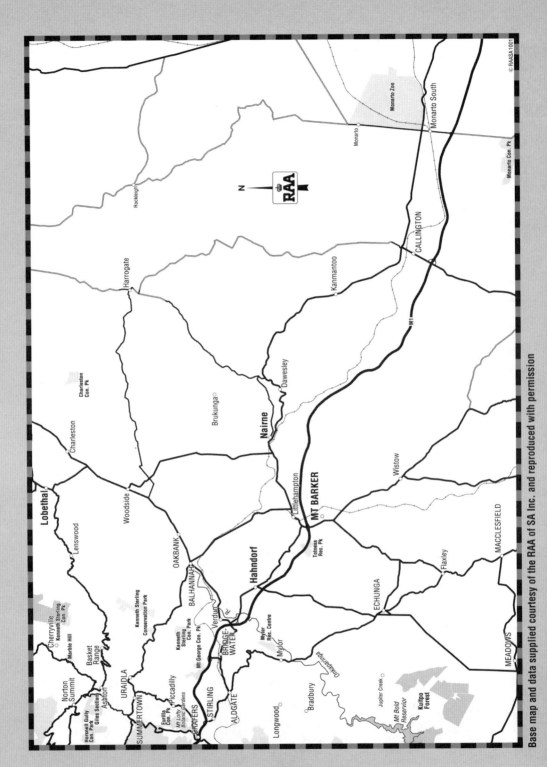

© RAASA1001

Base map and data supplied courtesy of the RAA of SA Inc. and reproduced with permission

Reverse: Keith at Mt Lofty Lookout Photo by Jeff Clayfield

From the giant gum landscape of Hans Heysen country around Hahndorf to the tiered vineyards of the fastest growing wine region in Australia, the Adelaide Hills provide a range of experiences. Colonel William Light called them 'the enchanted hills' and now we know why. You can walk through thick scrub, cruise through farming country, taste an excess of fabulous local wine and food over a lazy lunch, or wind across the Mount Lofty Ranges from one charming town to another.

The Adelaide Hills are so near to the city, yet so far without a car – until recently, that is. The Belair passenger train now joins with a weekend Hills Circle Link Bus for a do-it-yourself day tour.

Rolling hills near Oakbank   Photo by Lisa McAskilll

Set off on a magic carpet ride that takes you on a sweep of the hills.

Even before we stepped on the coach, the old Belair Railway Station signal box beckoned. Keen volunteers maintain the mechanical levers and they explain the steam era's charms before you set off on a magic carpet ride that takes you on a sweep of the hills. The hourly weekend train service winds its way from the Adelaide Station to Belair where it connects to the three-hour circle route bus. The idea is that passengers can tarry for an hour or two at any of its twelve stops to enjoy the local attractions, and join the bus again to complete the loop back to the station.

The first stop is not far into Belair National Park, with its beautifully restored Old Government House that provided cool summer respite for Her Majesty's representatives in the 1860s and 1870s when it was surrounded by the Government Farm. You can tour the house on Sunday afternoons, and take an easy walk through South Australia's

oldest National Park ... before you catch the next bus that winds out of the gullies and up onto the pretty ridge road across to Mount Lofty.

... home and studio of the much-loved painter Sir Hans Heysen.

Around Mount Lofty Summit is a quartet of stops to tempt passengers. Try coffee with a view of Piccadilly Valley at Mount Lofty House, a nineteenth-century mansion, or a walk in the Mount Lofty Botanic Garden that spills down through stringybark forest into

The Cedars, Hahndorf   Photo by Peter Clayton

gullies of exotic colour. Then there's Cleland Wildlife Reserve on the slopes towards the city. From the summit itself, you gaze down on a wonderful 180-degree panorama of Adelaide and the coast beyond. The trip continues north to delightful Uraidla before winding back through Balhannah to the outskirts of Hahndorf. Here, the bus makes

Tips From the Crew

- Lisa suggests a weekend at the Adelaide Hills Country Cottages at Oakbank. You can choose from a range of beautiful cottages and houses, all set on a lush 200-acre farm with its own lake.

- Keith suggests lunch or a coffee at the Scenic Hotel at Norton Summit as you look out over Adelaide.

- Trevor recommends heading straight for the German bakeries at Hahndorf.

- Jeff says take some bread to feed the ducks at Mount Lofty Botanic Gardens.

- Ron recommends a dusk tour of Warrawong Sanctuary at Mylor for a 'wild' native Australian animal experience.

I Didn't Know That!

- Before the First World War, Birdwood was called Blumberg, which is German for 'hill of flowers'. It was renamed after Australian forces Commander General Sir William Birdwood.

another bevy of stops including Beerenberg Strawberry Farm, the Hahndorf Farm Barn and The Cedars, the family home and studio of the much-loved painter Sir Hans Heysen.

Some passengers will choose to stay on board the tour for a pleasant hills ramble and then spend all their 'off-bus' time in South Australia's most visited country town.

Hahndorf was established in 1839 by Silesian migrants who came to the new colony to escape religious persecution. Today you'll find new wineries, gourmet produce and a rich art heritage. From Hahndorf, passengers on the Circle Link are taken via pretty hills towns back to Belair Station for their return trip to Adelaide.

The tour is a great way to get to know just a few of the highlights of the Adelaide Hills. Of course, there's so much more to see! In the Torrens Valley, bushwalkers can trek the Heysen and Mawson Trails and explore Mount

The Bickley family at the Hahndorf Farm Barn

Crawford Forest. At Birdwood the National Motor Museum, on the site of an old flour mill, is a fascinating trip through our motoring history. And a stone's throw from Gumeracha, the Chain of Ponds Winery produces award-winning wines along with rustic alfresco lunches.

- In the 1850s, the Adelaide Hills was home to a group of bushrangers referred to as the Tiersman. They prowled around the Mount Lofty Ranges stealing cattle for sale in Adelaide, and by night they went to Crafers for their grog. Their building skills and bushcraft proved very handy to the Hills' settlers.

- Young Silesian women walked from Hahndorf to Adelaide to sell their farm produce during the 1840s.

- The Heysen Trail runs for almost two thousand kilometres, starting at Cape Jervis in the south, meandering past Hans Heysen's former home and studio in the Adelaide Hills before heading north to the Flinders Ranges.

- The 1841 Three Brothers Arms hotel in Macclesfield was a stopover for Cobb & Co. coaches travelling to the eastern colonies.

- Kuitpo Forest near Meadows is a five thousand hectare forest, perfect for bird-watching, walking and picnics. The Heysen Trail travels through here, too.

... be a 'petrol head' for a day ...

The Onkaparinga Valley is home to vineyards, orchards, farms and food producers. Udder Delights at Lobethal make exceptional cheeses to drool over. Nearby you can taste one of the many cool-climate wines now produced in the Adelaide Hills. Wine and cheese is a marriage made in heaven, but the Adelaide Hills region is a cornucopia offering much more food for body and soul. It's Adelaide's food larder and pivotal to South Australia's push to export fresh, premium-quality produce.

As you continue through the Onkaparinga Valley, you'll find apples, pears and other fruit and vegetables for sale in roadside stalls. And when you get to Oakbank, remember it's home to the Easter Racing Carnival, with its famous Great Eastern Steeplechase. The Motorcycle and Heritage Museum at Lobethal is a biker's dream. If you'd like to be a 'petrol head' for a day, try a visit here first.

The Adelaide Hills begin twenty minutes from Adelaide and there are hundreds of great places to visit, eat, stay and enjoy. Once again, we could only pick a few of them. But we could fill another ten books if we tried to list them all – and we just well might!

Marble Hill Ruins   Copyright Rosemary Baldasso

Want More Information?

SA Visitor and Travel Centre
1300 655 276

Adelaide Hills Visitor Information Centre
1800 353 323

Adelaide Hills website
www.visitadelaidehills.com.au

Adelaide Hills Wine Region
(08) 8389 9343

Adelaide Hills Circle Link Bus
(08) 8210 1000

National Parks and Wildlife SA
(08) 8204 1910

RAA Touring (maps and guides)
(08) 8205 4540

SA Tourism Commission website
www.southaustralia.com

***Postcards* website**
www.postcards.sa.com.au

The Cedars

with Ron Kandelaars

Sir Hans Heysen was never short of inspiration. From the studio window at the Heysen's Hahndorf property, The Cedars, every view was another painting waiting to be created. Inside the magnificent stone studio, perched in a paddock not far from the family home, everything remains as it was when he worked here, prior to his death in 1968. Footmarks on the studio floor, often referred to as the 'sacred spot', indicate where Heysen stood while painting. Two unfinished works sit by the window, and paints, easels, and tools of his trade line the shelves.

Hans Heysen arrived in Australia from Hamburg, Germany, in 1884 as a six-year-old, and immediately fell in love with the strangeness of the Australian bush, especially his beloved Adelaide Hills. Heysen's enchantment with nature helped to change the way Australians viewed their world. During his illustrious career many of his paintings were sold to galleries and private collections throughout Australia and overseas, and they remain prized works of art today.

Heysen lived to paint and art was everything to him – although, an incident during the war years brought home the realisation that everything is political, even in the world of art. The Victorian Gallery had earmarked one of Heysen's works for purchase, but promptly cancelled the deal when they learned of his German background. Heysen never forgot this, and it left an indelible mark on him.

In turn, his work left an indelible mark on those who considered our natural landscape ugly and colourless. Thanks in part to Heysen and other painters, Australians gradually began to see their landscape as truly unique and beautiful. That's the feeling you get from the scene in Heysen's evocative painting *The Way Home* which shows Heysen's favourite model, old man Collins, in Billy Goat Lane, Hahndorf, in 1908. Hans used to pay Collins a shilling to walk down a road or sit under a gum tree, and the old man quickly became a village celebrity.

Hans and his wife, Sallie, lived in the village of Hahndorf for four years until 1912, when they realised their dream of a beautiful country property and moved up the road to The Cedars. Here they raised a brood of children, grew fruit and vegetables, and tended chickens and cows – a self-sufficient lifestyle that helped them through some difficult times. The house was often full of visitors including politicians, dancers, musicians, and the rich and famous, who all came to buy Heysen's paintings. The couple lived in the family home throughout their married life.

Heysen's magnificent stone studio is set in a paddock not far from the family home

The Cedars is still owned by the Heysen family, and they've now installed on the property a series of lift-up panels called the Artist's Walk. Each panel marks a spot where Heysen painted and gives details of his work. As you travel the property by foot, you realise how much of Sir Hans' inspiration came from his own back yard.

Heysen was also one of the first artists to capture the rugged beauty of inland Australia. His trusty 'A' Model Ford and van are still parked in the shed at The Cedars, as a reminder of his many painting expeditions to the Flinders Ranges.

Nora Heysen was the only one of Heysen's eight children to follow in her father's footsteps. She enrolled at the North Adelaide School of Fine Arts at the age of fifteen, and within five years, had paintings in three State Galleries. As a twenty-seven-year-old she became the first woman to win the Archibald Prize for portraiture. At The Cedars you can also see a selection of Nora's paintings.

Step inside the two-storey family home on one of Allan Campbell's guided tours and wander room after room, each filled with Hans Heysen's works. One such piece, *Zinneas and Autumn Fruit*, now hangs above the fireplace in the sitting room. It so captivated the great Russian ballerina Pavlova on one of her visits that she simply had to have it – she wrote out a blank cheque on the spot. But the painting had been a gift from Heysen to his wife, and he refused to sell it. He painted another similar piece and sent it to Pavlova in Europe. She promptly returned it, replying that only the original would do! This is just one of the many stories you'll hear on your hour-long tour of the property. It's worth a visit to the Hills just to see it.

The Cedars

Heysen Road, Hahndorf
South Australia 5245
Tel (08) 8388 7277
Open every day except Saturday.
Viewing by guided tour.

Marble Hill Ruins

with Keith Conlon

Marble Hill is now a grand skeleton
of a mansion   Copyright Wendy Mack

High in the Mount Lofty Ranges looms a romantic tragedy of a ruin. It took just hours for the cruel Black Sunday bushfire in 1955 to gut Marble Hill. What remains is a grand skeleton of a mansion.

The governor's new summer residence was ready to greet Lieutenant Governor Sir William Jervois and his party for the New Year of 1880. 'Victorian academic gothic' in style and built of local stone, Marble Hill was designed by prominent architect William McMinn, who also gave us the gothic Mitchell Building at Adelaide University and the decorative Austral Hotel in Rundle Street.

For seventy-five years Marble Hill was the holiday home of South Australia's Governors, offering a cool retreat from the heat of the Adelaide plains. Well, most of the time. It was first threatened by bushfires a century ago when Lady Tennyson wrote 'our own gully garden is on fire'. In 1912 another blaze licked close enough to char the rosary and crack some windows. The arrival of the English cricket team, who had been invited for dinner, saved the day – the Poms were conscripted to beat the fire back.

Lady Tennyson loved the 'delightful huge verandahs' that offered shade on sizzling days and protection in freezing winters – once, in 1908, it snowed here for three days. But summer's dangers always lurked: the Black Friday bushfires first threatened the hilltop house in 1939.

Wandering along the walkways through the ruin, we can only imagine what Marble Hill's twenty-six rooms looked like. There are photos of the spacious dining room and the comfortable morning room, but even the great bay window of the drawing room is gone now. The great hall gapes skyward where there was once a beautifully carved kauri pine staircase turning up to a row of gothic arches.

The Country Fire Service now uses the restored mansion tower as a lookout, but even this fine band of volunteers would have been powerless against the Black Sunday bushfire on 2 January 1955. A gale pushed a raging fire up the ridge, and Marble Hill's caretaker reported that 'the blaze was upon them with the speed of an express train'. Fifteen people including the Governor, Sir Robert George, his wife and two children were in residence. As they watched, the heat melted the lead lining on the tower roof and showered down to cover the cars below. Miraculously, all the residents survived. They rushed to a high retaining wall on the laurel-hedged drive and sheltered under blankets until help came. But the Marble Hill mansion was razed.

Within months, the state government declared it would never be rebuilt. And forty-six years later there is still no chance. Thanks, however, to the Friends of Marble Hill, the remnant is preserved and regularly open to us all. Volunteers are usually on hand during open days to explain some macabre remains.

If you're seeking more cheerful sights, head up to the top of the tower. It projects about six storeys up from the high vantage point chosen for Marble Hill. On a clear day, the view spans a good 150 kilometres – Mount Lofty and the ranges beyond Echunga to the south, the gnarled and heavy scrub of the ranges close by across a deep gully to the east and the Barossa Range and the distant Hummocks beyond Port Wakefield.

The *Register*'s nineteenth century reports were correct. This view is 'a romantic panorama of surpassing loveliness'. The tower is open whenever the property is staffed by the Friends and they'll sell you a light lunch or scones from the coachhouse around the hill from the mansion. The coachhouse is now restored and used for weddings and functions.

Marble Hill Road
(20 kilometres from Adelaide
via Montacute Road), Ashton
South Australia 5137
Tel (08) 8390 0414
Open second Sunday of each month.

Marble Hill
Ruins

Monarto Zoological Park
with Keith Conlon

The wildlife comes right into the car park! As we were setting up for our Monarto Zoological Park shoot, the *Postcards* crew watched a brood of a dozen emu chicks squat around a puddle to share a drink. Spring is a perfect time to experience Monarto's different faces. It's both a breeding and educational zoological park, and a natural Australian wilderness area as well.

Monarto wouldn't have happened if it weren't for a 1970s folly. An ill-fated satellite city of the same name was planned for these shallow farm valleys and mallee ridge-tops. Instead, just an hour's drive from Adelaide, herds of endangered beasts from Africa and Asia now roam in giant enclosures over its one thousand hectares.

Everyone starts at the Visitor Centre, a striking galvanised-iron and timber structure that has picked up architectural awards. From there you climb aboard a zoo bus, unless you'd prefer to take the guided walk first.

The mallee-scrub ridges are a great place for a walk and they're particularly beautiful in spring. In some places, regeneration has allowed the land to regain its natural health and you'll find scatterings of sheoaks and native pines, along with great spreads of native flowers. Mallee, which once was knocked over to make way for sheep-grazing, is again providing a shady gum-leaf canopy in parts. The sound of bush birds is everywhere. We saw a family feeding its young in a smooth clay nest, an eaglet high in a mallee-tree stick nest, and another emu with his brood, foraging through the leaf-litter.

On the bus tour through the green paddocks, you drive across two continents in about an hour. In the Asian grasslands, the living ancestors of buffalo and cattle, the nilgai, graze unperturbed. Smaller blackbuck Indian antelopes add a dash of athleticism and 'pronk' as the bus passes by – that's the name for those startling four-legged leaps

Opposite top: At Monarto Zoological Park, visitors are caged in buses while the animals run free
Copyright Grant Nowell   Opposite bottom: Cheetahs, originally from a South African breeding reserve,
now roam in the Australian bush   Wildside Photography

into the air. Through another gate, and you're into living fossil country where American bison and Mongolian wild horses are back together again after twenty thousand years. They once featured in Palaeolithic artists' cave paintings.

On board the bus, the conversation about the breeding program is entertaining – and compulsory. At Monarto, visitors are caged in buses while the animals run free. Chapman's zebra halt progress as they pay scant regard for the oncoming bus. The largest of the antelopes, the eland, are more circumspect, trotting away as a herd. On the other hand, the giraffe group will usually wander over for a closer look.

We were keen to get pictures of the baby giraffe. She obliged, tottering awkwardly in the golden afternoon light. Her father, Kutabe, also enjoyed the cameras. He came right up to the back of our open four-wheel-drive and gave the lens a kiss! Our sound recordist, Trevor, who loves giraffes, found himself cheek-to-cheek – and Kutabe has a very big cheek.

Cheetahs, originally from a South African breeding reserve, now roam in the Australian bush at Monarto. Their neighbours in the next paddock are white rhinos and more giraffes. Over the next mallee rise are lions and cape hunting dogs, and behind the old wheat farm buildings, the Australian Conservation Centre continues to breed indigenous animals like bilbies, bettongs, bandicoots and more.

Don't worry if you can't make it in spring: Monarto provides an amazing experience all year round. It's about seventy kilometres from Adelaide. Tours start from half past ten each morning from the Visitor Centre. If you don't want to take the car, then a bus leaves the Central Bus Station in Franklin Street each weekday morning at nine. As part of the total package you can join the Monarto Tour and be back in Adelaide by quarter to two.

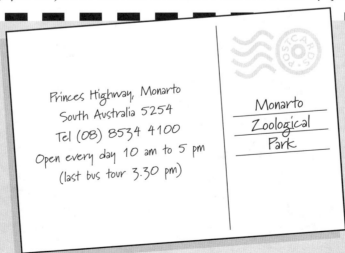

Princes Highway, Monarto
South Australia 5254
Tel (08) 8534 4100
Open every day 10 am to 5 pm
(last bus tour 3.30 pm)

Monarto
Zoological
Park

Lavendula

with Mike Keelan

The garden at Lavendula is meandering and uncontrived

Your average nineteenth-century police station with cells was normally a dour affair. And that's precisely what the Callington Police Station was – at least until garden designer and interior decorator Chris Wilkinson got her hands on it. Built in 1867, the station operated until the turn of the century and its cells offered short-term accommodation for petty criminals back in the days when Callington was a boisterous copper-mining town.

Today, Chris has transformed the old police station into a distinctive house, cafe and garden called Lavendula. The garden at Lavendula is meandering and uncontrived, as if someone threw a packet of seeds into the air to see how they would fall: nasturtium, salvia, erigeron, phlox, fine leaf, broad leaf, big and small, all tossed in together. And that's the way Chris thinks it should be.

'But isn't that nature? It isn't in straight lines. It's like, what's around the corner there? Everything you do, you must have passion for, because you become very daring when you have passion. You don't think about whether it's right or proper, you just say, this is it.'

For Chris, designing a garden is all about taking hold of emotions buried deep within.

'With all due respect to the experts, forget what they say in the main. Just say, Now what do I love? Close your eyes. What brings back good memories, what perfumes are involved with happy thoughts in your life?'

Around the corner, another garden contains an underground water tank, a pre-requisite here at Callington where the rainfall is half that of Adelaide. But that hasn't stopped Chris from creating a colourful display to gaze upon while you enjoy Devonshire tea or a light lunch in her cafe. She says:

'I'm not presuming that it looks anything like Monet's garden, but impressionist painters come here and use these lovely subtle colours, like a tapestry, then the iris come out in the spring ... You can definitely say there is a French connection here.'

The interior of the old police station is now Chris Wilkinson's home, and it reflects the same unordered approach. There's no ornate Victorian stencilling here, rather a free-and-easy approach to decorating, in the manner of a French farmhouse. Here, and in the gardens, Chris conducts her all-day seminars called 'Decorating on a Shoe String Budget'. Lavendula is open for lunches and afternoon teas from Thursday to Sunday and you'll find the Old Callington Police Station on Montefiore Street, Callington.

Old Callington Police Station
Montefiore Street, Callington
South Australia 5254
Tel (08) 8538 5138
Open Thursday to Sunday.

Lavendula

Jupiter Creek Gold Mine
with Ron Kandelaars

You see them everywhere, eternal optimists with metal detectors convinced that a major find is just a sweep away. As you wander through the Jupiter Creek Gold Fields near Echunga, you realise that the Adelaide Hills are alive with the sound of fossicking.

For a fossicker like Andrew Ennis, one man's rubbish may be another man's fortune as he picks over mine-workings dating back to the 1860s when the Jupiter Creek field experienced its own mini-gold rush:

'This is an old shaft here with a mullock heap. The old-timers would have dug that hole and thrown the dirt in this pile here. They didn't have the advantage of metal detectors back in those days, so any gold that wasn't obvious went onto the heap.'

The Jupiter Creek fields produced some of the best gold in South Australia

Just as the early diggers here had to contend with a daily diet of expectation and frustration, our crew's hopes were shattered when our 'find' turned out to be a rusty tobacco tin left over from the old mining days. Anyone can fossick here as long as they fill in their workings. In a quiet way, the gold rush never ended here thanks to fossickers like Andrew – or the *Postcards* crew! – trying their luck among the stringybarks and wattles or panning at Battery Creek.

The Beatrice Mining Company was formed in 1868 and its Cornish-style round-stone chimney remains a significant relic of the gold-mining days. No doubt the itinerant diggers who were doing it tough in the nearby creek envied the power of the great battery – a crusher powered by a large steam engine. Only a third found enough to make wages, and so the first rush was short-lived. But they were back again in the 1930s Depression, picking over the Jupiter Creek fields just as we were. Back then the technology involved picks and dynamite and the Depression miners have left a remarkable legacy, the New Phoenix Shaft, a tunnel cut horizontally into the side of the hill towards the old Phoenix Mine. Andrew Ennis says that the mine produced some of the best gold in South Australia, with around eight thousand ounces found in this area. 'And there's still some left today,' says Andrew, 'fossickers are finding material all the time.'

Andrew's Adelaide shop, the Miners Den, is living proof that 'there's gold in them thar hills'. Here he displays specimens found on his fossicking trips, including a seven-and-a-half-ounce nugget. Many who come into the store find themselves swept away by gold fever and are soon taking part in Andrew's regular courses and tours of the gold fields. Others scour nearby beaches in search of more common lost treasure.

Now and again, Andrew gets an unusual request:

'One chap rang up and said he'd had a fight with the missus, spat the dummy and threw the wedding ring over the back fence. He needed a metal detector to find it.'

Whether it's to save a marriage or uncover a small fortune, the metal detectors at the Miners Den come in a range of sizes and are available for hire. Andrew also runs regular courses and tours. The Jupiter Creek Gold Mines are open to the public for fossicking.

Jupiter Creek
Gold Mine

Off Berry Road, Echunga
South Australia 5153
Tel (08) 8463 3000

The
Miner's Den

162 Grange Road, Flinders Park
South Australia 5025
Tel (08) 8340 3633

Fleurieu Peninsula

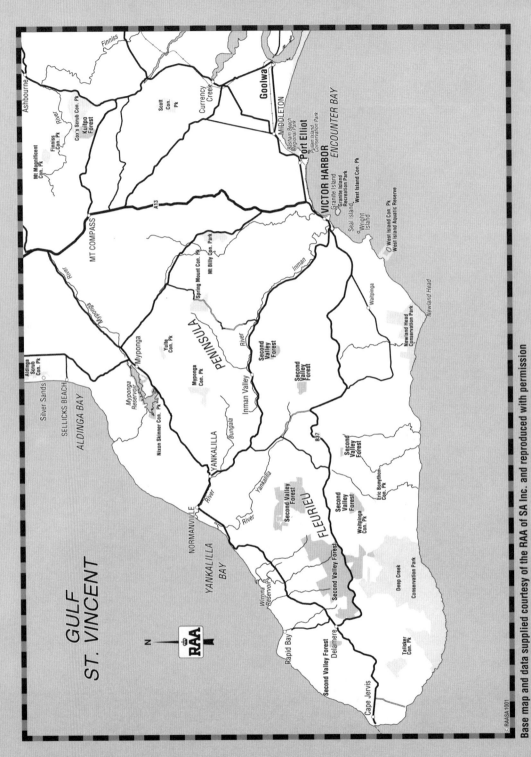

GULF
ST. VINCENT

N

RAA

YANKALILLA BAY

ALDINGA BAY

Silver Sands

SELLICKS BEACH

Aldinga Scrub Con. Pk

NORMANVILLE

YANKALILLA

Nixon Skinner Con. Pk

Myponga Reservoir

Myponga

Myponga Con. Pk

Yulte Con. Pk

PENINSULA

Inman Valley

Bungala

MT COMPASS

Spring Mount Con. Pk

Mt Billy Con. Park

Second Valley Forest

Second Valley Forest

Inman

Waitpinga

Newland Head

Newland Head Conservation Park

MIDDLETON

Goolwa

Currency Creek

Scott Con. Pk

Cox's Scrub Con. Pk

Kuitpo Forest

Finniss

River

Finniss Con. Pk

Mt Magnificent Con. Pk

Ashbourne

A13

A327

Port Elliot

Basham Beach Regional Park

VICTOR HARBOR

Granite Island
Granite Island Recreation Park

Seal Island

Wright Island

West Island Con. Pk

West Island Con. Pk
West Island Aquatic Reserve

Pullen Island Conservation Park

ENCOUNTER BAY

Rapid Bay

Second Valley Forest

Delamere

Cape Jervis

FLEURIEU

Second Valley Forest

Second Valley Forest

Second Valley Forest

Second Valley Forest

Second Valley Forest

Waitpinga Con. Pk

Eric Bonython Con. Pk

Deep Creek Conservation Park

Talisker Con. Pk

B37

Yankalilla River

Wirrina Reservoir

C-RASA1001

Base map and data supplied courtesy of the RAA of SA Inc. and reproduced with permission

Reverse: Deep Creek Conservation Park   Photo by Bernd Stoecker

For many Adelaide families, the annual migration to the Fleurieu, cars stacked up high with boogie boards, beach umbrellas and bait, is as natural as the change of the seasons. Every summer, the coastal towns swell with hoards of holiday-makers and the local businesses get their cash registers ready. Cafes and restaurants offering tantalising local food, a medley of cellar doors to explore in one of the many wine-producing regions, an excellent range of holiday accommodation from camping to luxury bed and breakfasts, historic towns, boating, fishing, surfing and swimming – all combine to give the Fleurieu its wonderful 'sea and vines' flavour.

The Fleurieu Peninsula was named by Nicholas Baudin, the French explorer who met up with English navigator Matthew Flinders near the Murray Mouth in 1802, thirty years or so before the colony of South Australia was established. The French and the English were at war, but the explorers' meeting was apparently not marred by the politics of the time.

Wooden Boat Festival, Goolwa   Photo by Keith Conlon   Steam-powered Cockle Train   Photo by Keith Conlon

The Ngarrindjeri nation was divided into eighteen clans,
each with their own government and lands.

Two distinct Aboriginal groups, the Kaurna and the Ngarrindjeri, lived in various, well-defined parts of the region at the time of colonisation. Both groups had sophisticated social structures, many thousands of years old. The Ngarrindjeri nation was divided into eighteen clans, each with their own government and lands. The rich land and sea of the peninsula offered an abundance of food and raw materials for clothing, hunting implements, transport and housing. Although many of the Kaurna were wiped out by colonisation, their culture has survived. The Ngarrindjeri culture also continues, with a strong weaving and fishing tradition still evident today. You can experience and learn about the Ngarrindjeri people first-hand at Camp Coorong south of Meningie.

This 'off the beaten track' route is definitely worth the extra hour or more it takes to get there.

The Fleurieu is a majestic place to visit and explore. When you're heading south to popular Victor Harbor, try the road less travelled. As you head along South Road go past the Victor turn-off and you'll drift among wonderful velvety hills, lush pastures, scrubby rises, roads carved into cliffs that twist and wind before revealing magnificent postcard views of the coastline and delightful valleys that lead to quiet coves.

Deep Creek Cove   Photo by Bernd Stoecker

By now, you've passed through rural Yankalilla, past the beachfront shacks of Lady Bay, through Second Valley and you're heading towards Delamere. Although this is the main route from Adelaide to the Kangaroo Island ferry at Cape Jervis, the valleys retain a peaceful, rural feel. At Delamere you can turn left and head along a stunning ridge past Deep Creek Conservation Park and on towards Victor Harbor.

We can't guarantee a quick drive with this 'off the beaten track' route to Victor, but it's definitely worth the extra hour or

Tips From the Crew

- Jeff says catch the Flying Fish Cafe at Port Elliot. You can have lunch or coffee while you gaze out over beautiful Horseshoe Bay. He also suggests a pasty crawl of the famous bakeries in Port Elliot, Middleton and Goolwa.

- Ron recommends Surf Culture Australia's surfing lessons held at Middleton. You might even be able to stand up when you're finished!

- Lisa suggests a sunset drive to the Murray Mouth on Hindmarsh Island.

- Mike says head down to Deep Creek Conservation Park in the late afternoon. You'll find a crowd of huge grey kangaroos to keep you company.

- Trevor says the Whistle Stop Cafe at Goolwa is wonderful. The food is great and the cafe brims with fabulous curios and antiques.

- Keith recommends a walk into the beautiful Onkaparinga Gorge – a touch of the Flinders in our southern suburbs.

more it takes to get there. If you decide to go past Delamere towards Cape Jervis, you'll soon find the turn-off to the old tin mines at the Talisker Conservation Park. While you're down that way, keep an eye out for spectacular glimpses of the coastline.

Its seams burst with a migrating population in summer.

The holiday towns of Victor Harbor, Port Elliot, Middleton and Goolwa are all dotted along the coast from The Bluff's amazing coastal views to the Murray Mouth where the river meets the sea. While Victor Harbor is a favourite retirement spot and serene in winter, its seams burst with a migrating population in summer. The neighbouring towns are all in the same boat, but the locals don't seem to mind the onslaught. A bevy of welcoming cafes, restaurants, pubs and attractions open their doors to the vacationing hoards, as their ship comes in.

Signal Point River Murray Interpretive Centre at Goolwa is a good place

Allusion winery, Yankalilla

I Didn't Know That!

- Maslin Beach, Australia's first proclaimed nudist beach, plays host to the Nudist Olympics every January.

- Sir Douglas Mawson, the famous Antarctic explorer, lived in the Meadows district during the 1920s.

- At Port Willunga the wreck of the cargo ship *Star of Greece* is still visible at low tide. A walk along the beautiful beach reveals pylons from the old jetty that was destroyed by a storm in 1915. While you're there, try lunch at the cliff-top Star of Greece cafe.

- In the early days of colonisation Colonial William Light landed at Rapid Bay and carved his initials and the date on a boulder. The boulder, along with a monument, can still be seen today.

- The southern right whale was so named because it floated when it was killed. This made it 'right'.

- You'll find Selwyn's Glacier Rock, one of the largest glacial exposures in the world, at Inman Valley.

- Every year thousands visit the Anglican Church at Yankalilla to view the 'Madonna and Child' silhouette on the interior wall there.

- As well as being a fantastic surf beach, Waitpinga Beach is a great spot for salmon fishing.

to start your education of the area's rich river-boat history. At Goolwa's annual Wooden Boat Festival you'll find a fantastic line up of glossy wooden boats (and their devoted owners) from all over Australia. Down by the Goolwa Wharf you can hop on board the steam-powered Cockle Train for a noisy, scenic ride to Victor Harbor and return.

You can wander all over the Fleurieu in search of your favourite wine, from the pretty and renowned McLaren Vale region to the Middleton, Rapid Bay, Currency Creek, Langhorne Creek, Finniss and Yankalilla wine-producers. And along with fabulous wines come platters of local olives, almonds, avocados, stone fruit and cheese giving the region a Mediterranean flavour. Regional celebrations like the 'Sea and Vines' and the 'Willunga Almond Blossom' revel in the region's local produce and sense of community.

Close proximity to Adelaide means that you can experience the wonders of the Fleurieu Peninsula in a series of day trips, or plan to stay longer and luxuriate in the holiday atmosphere. From wine to maritime history to a bike ride along the coast, our *Postcards* stories reflect the diversity of this lively retreat. So enjoy ... and visit the Fleurieu soon.

Xanthorrhoea at Sunset Blowhole Photo by Volker Scholz

Want More Information?

SA Visitor and Travel Centre
1300 655 276

Fleurieu Peninsula website
www.fleurieupeninsula.com.au

McLaren Vale and Fleurieu Visitor Centre
(08) 8323 9944

Victor Harbor Information Centre
(08) 8552 5738

Goolwa Information Centre
(08) 8555 1144

National Parks and Wildlife SA
(08) 8552 3677

RAA Touring (maps and guides)
(08) 8205 4540

SA Tourism Commission website
www.southaustralia.com.au

***Postcards* website**
www.postcards.sa.com.au

Encounter Bikeway

with Keith Conlon

Old stone farm outhouses and a dairy provide shelter on the Encounter Bikeway

Photo courtesy SA Tourism Commission

Encounter Bay is a legendary holiday region for South Australians, thanks to spectacular surf beaches, a strong sense of history and leviathan visitors in winter. Now there is a new way of experiencing it all. I mounted a hired bicycle for a twenty-kilometre-plus easy ride all the way from The Bluff at Victor Harbor to Goolwa, the once-mighty river port at the mouth of the Murray.

After a run between the Norfolk Pines, the path swaps seascapes for glimpses of nature as it detours around the pretty Inman River estuary, past rare swamp paperbarks and a host of native waterbirds. The game and the native plants made this an attractive semi-permanent camping area for the local Aboriginal people, who wove the reeds into baskets, nets and shelter.

A short ride along the Victor Harbor esplanade brings a smorgasbord of tempting detours as you cycle up to the famous horse tram that crosses the causeway to

Granite Island. The 300 metre Granite Island breakwater was a nineteenth-century engineering marvel that helped turn Victor Harbor into a major port.

Between Victor Harbor and Port Elliot, the pathway sticks close to the Cockle Train line along the top of the steep sandhills. The train runs between Victor Harbor and Goolwa on Australia's oldest railway dating back to 1854. The picturesque views back to Victor and The Bluff have enchanted stream train passengers for generations.

A slight deviation to Freeman Nob is a must. Sylvester Freeman was a whaler who kept lookout from this promontory. The whalers' prey was all but gone when the aptly named Horseshoe Bay below was declared an official port and the tall obelisk on the Nob went up in 1852 to beckon incoming sailing ships. Port Elliot thrived briefly on shipping cargo coming down the River Murray on paddlesteamers and then across to the town on Australia's first iron-tracked railway.

On our recent *Postcards* shoot, Horseshoe Bay was a placid spot for a paddle, but 1856 was a black and stormy year. Four ships were wrecked in the ill-protected cove.

The long esplanade ride offers endless views of the pounding breakers of the Southern Ocean

The port proved so dangerous that the railway line was pushed through to Port Victor by the 1860s, and Port Elliot lost its job. A meander through the town reveals a cluster of buildings harking back to this bustling era.

Come the winter, and the bikeway will give you mobile viewing of the giant southern right whales. They love the strip of bay beyond Basham's Beach on the way to the holiday town of Middleton. Old stone farm outhouses and a dairy provide shelter on the trail as it sweeps through the paddocks behind the windswept sandhills.

Middleton itself is really two towns. The bikeway clings to the coast where the holiday house subdivisions of the last fifty years are still growing, while the nineteenth-century village spans the old railway line up the rise. The long esplanade ride here is softened by endless views of the rolling and pounding breakers of the Southern Ocean.

At the Goolwa end of Middleton, the Encounter Bikeway swings inland into a far less-travelled place. In a nice act of collaboration, Ngarrindjeri groups and the Alexandrina Council have let us into the last wetland eco-system in these parts, the

Photo courtesy SA Tourism Commission

Tokuremoar Conservation Park. The path snakes past tall and ancient paperbarks and then enters a boardwalk that weaves through a swampy forest. The raised wooden track protects the delicate ground vegetation and brings you quietly into close viewing of the tiny fairy wrens, stilts, egrets and more.

From here it's an easy ride through the holiday houses that stretch to the sea from Goolwa. The great elbow of the Murray that gave the port its name, provides the backdrop for the last part of the bike ride. The Goolwa Yacht Club, the boardwalk marinas and then a historic river wharf are all worthy photographic shots. A modern paddle-steamer has become a floating motel, one of many choices of accommodation at this end. And beyond is the historic town of Goolwa, the wooden boat capital of the world. The newly opened and controversial Hindmarsh Island bridge that arcs high over the old riverboat dock now provides the means to extend your bike ride all the way to the Murray Mouth.

A new brochure on the bikeway is available from the Signal Point Interpretive Centre across the railway line at the Goolwa wharf and there are bike hire shops in Victor Harbor and Goolwa. On weekends, you can make it a one-way ride by putting your bikes on the Cockle Train for the return trip. Riding the Encounter Bikeway is an invigorating way to rediscover the many charms of this popular coastline, and I hope you too soon get rolling along it. Happy Trails.

Encounter Bikeway brochures available from Signal Point The Wharf, Goolwa, South Australia 5124, tel (08) 8555 3488. Open every day 9 am–5 pm except Christmas Day.

Brochures also from:
Victor Harbor Information Centre
The Causeway, Victor Harbor
South Australia 5211
Tel (08) 8552 5738
Open every day 9 am–5pm

Encounter
Bikeway

Allusion Wines
with Lisa McAskill

About an hour's drive south of Adelaide, you can lose yourself in hidden, lush valleys between Yankalilla and Normanville. And that's just what winemaker Steve Taylor decided to do when he returned to Australia from France over a decade ago. Steve lost himself in a south coast valley and set about fulfilling a dream:

'I was working as a chef in the Loire Valley in France and we came back and wanted to produce authentic, single-vineyard, regional wines, much as they do over there.'

While touring the country markets of France and sampling their wares along the road, Steve and his wife, Wendy, developed a healthy appetite for regional food and wines. Now, in his own quiet valley, Steve is staging a personal crusade against the onslaught of globalisation:

'We fell in love with the regionality of the wine and food that we savoured over there and had this dream of coming back to this part of the peninsula and doing the same thing. In this day and age of global wines and global food, I wanted people to know that what they buy from here comes from our soil and is made with love and passion.'

Netting on the vines guards against marauding parrots at Allusion Wines. Every drop of juice from these grapes is vital; there's no blending here. And, according to Steve, there's no need to blend or tamper with the variety nature has provided:

Steve Taylor at Allusion Wines' cellar door

'This area was glacial millions of years ago, and as the glacier was heading down the valley, it pushed this little hill that we're on up ahead of itself and then diverted down the Carrakalinga Creek, to Carrakalinga itself. Consequently, we've got about five different soil types here. We have each variety of plant on a different type of soil to create the optimum growing conditions for those varieties. So our whites tend to be slightly flinty. Our cab is a big beast and our shiraz is looking exciting.'

From the kitchen window of the winery you can see the blue waters of Gulf St Vincent. Steve's passion for the possibilities of his own back yard stem from the fact that he once nearly lost sight of all of this. In fact, he was almost consumed by it. Out boating with a couple of friends one day, they were forced to abandon their twenty-three foot cabin cruiser and swim to shore after huge waves driven by gale force winds swamped and sank it. The trio spent more than an hour in freezing water battling five-metre waves to reach land. They became separated in the swell and all three men feared their mates would not live.

Steve nearly lost his life near where another small vessel, the *Allusion*, sank off the coast of Kangaroo Island years ago. Now the wine label is a reminder of a moment in time that caused this young winemaker to re-evaluate his life:

'For me, there's no question about it. I want to have time to enjoy my family and my dreams. I've never worked so hard in my life, but we love it, it gives us time with each other and we can follow our dream.'

Smith Road, Yankalilla
South Australia 5203
Tel (08) 8558 3333
Open on weekends 11 am—5 pm
or by appointment

Allusion
Wines

Deep Creek Conservation Park
with Ron Kandelaars

Just ninety minutes south of Adelaide lies the four-and-a-half-thousand hectare Deep Creek Conservation Park. It's the largest portion of unspoilt natural vegetation on the Fleurieu Peninsula, with around eighteen kilometres of majestic coastline.

The park is named after a small creek that slices its way through thick scrub and low-lying heath country. It also winds its way through beautiful stringybark forests, havens for the yellow-tailed black cockatoo and Adelaide rosella. In fact, this stretch of thick stringybark is one of the most pristine in South Australia, having been logged only for a short period during the Second World War. As you leave the stringybark and make for the coast the flora slowly changes to dense woodland.

A world-famous walking track, the Heysen Trail, and a number of shorter walks snake their way through almost twenty kilometres of the park, offering spectacular coastal views of an island

Deep Creek Conservation Park is named after a small creek that slices its way through thick scrub and low-lying heath country   Photo by Volker Scholz

Conservation Park The Pages, and further out to Kangaroo Island. The views are enticing but remember that walking here requires decent preparation and gear.

It's not hard to see why Deep Creek is such a magnet for bushwalkers and campers. Kangaroos abound in the open country, along with a host of smaller mammals. Deep Creek is a coastal park, and there's a good chance you will see dolphins, seals and the occasional whale.

Five camping grounds are located throughout the park, while if you want a more luxurious holiday, Southern Ocean Retreats operates a number of cottages throughout Deep Creek, including the Deep Creek Homestead. The day we arrived at the Homestead, we were greeted by mobs of kangaroos. Stay here overnight and you'll see plenty of birds and animals as you walk around the park during the day, you'll be surrounded by them at night and they'll be there in the morning when you wake up.

The Homestead was built for a returned serviceman who took up residence in 1946. For many years the property was used to run sheep and cattle, and was later acquired by the National Parks and Wildlife Service as part of the park. For twenty years the homestead was abandoned and required major restoration work. Now its jarrah floorboards stand out as a feature – along with its beautiful views.

To get to Deep Creek drive past Second Valley and turn left at the Delamere Store, then follow the signs to the Park Headquarters.

Southern Ocean Retreats
Tel (08) 8598 4169

Deep Creek
Homestead

Tel (08) 8598 0263

Deep Creek
Conservation
Park

Yelki by the Sea
with Lisa McAskill

Y ou could easily pass by this classic piece of South Australian history. It's nestled on the shore of Encounter Bay as if in retreat from the modern world, content to remember this area as it was one-hundred-and-sixty years ago. Yelki by the Sea is now a cosy bed and breakfast, but back then it was the first hotel at Encounter Bay. Soon after the establishment of the South Australian Company's whaling station under the Bluff it was known as the Ship Inn and, by all accounts, was a rough and ready place.

By day the whalers scoured this part of the Fleurieu in search of southern right whales, doing their bit for the state's first export industry. By night, they'd come around the back of the Ship Inn to fill up on rum. They were a boisterous lot – hard working, hard drinking, often violent, and many were escaped convicts. The front section of the inn, which provided accommodation for paying guests, was off limits to the whaling rabble. When they'd had their fill of rum, the publican herded up to twenty of them at a time into a small windowless building away from the main inn.

The charming Yelki by the Sea

It would have made for an uncomfortable night's sleep, particularly in summer. Come morning, weary whalers with savage hangovers could keep a bleary-eyed watch on the nearby Bluff. If a flag was raised, a whale had been sighted, and it was time to get back to work.

As the town of Victor Harbor expanded, so too did the pub. In 1847 it was renamed the Fountain Inn. It continued to be a favourite haunt of the whaling community until the 1850s, by when the whales had been nearly hunted to extinction along this coast. The last one – at least until their recent return – was towed into The Bluff in 1872.

The pub lived on until the 1890s, when Reverend James Jefferis bought it as his family's holiday retreat and renamed it Yelki. Reverend Jefferis played a key role in the establishment of Adelaide University and was a founder of one of the city's other landmarks, the Congregational Church at North Adelaide. But probably his greatest contribution was as a driving force for nationhood, as he pushed for the loose collection of colonies to federate into a new Commonwealth of Australia.

In the reverend's later years, it was a case of moving everything lock stock and barrel down from Adelaide for the annual summer holiday. Reports say he used to bring his wife and thirteen children, their chooks, and a cow with him on the train to the holiday house.

Yelki by the Sea remains a charming holiday retreat with an unconventional history – but please don't bring the chooks.

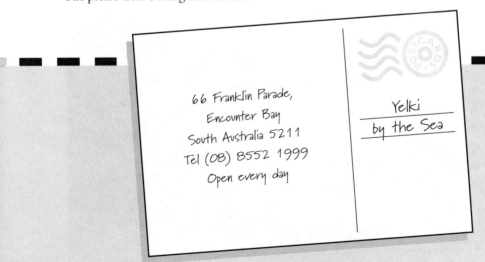

66 Franklin Parade,
Encounter Bay
South Australia 5211
Tel (08) 8552 1999
Open every day

Yelki
by the Sea

Goolwa Maritime Gallery
with Ron Kandelaars

Some obsessions pass like the waves, but Chris and Judy Crabtree's devotion to all things nautical has lasted a lifetime. Chris and Judy have charted their own special course away from the city rat-race to the banks of the Murray at Goolwa, opposite Hindmarsh Island, where they live on a converted 1880s tugboat.

On the riverbank, not far from their floating home, Chris and Judy have transformed an 1880s Chart Room, once used to store plans for paddle-steamers and other rivercraft, into a museum of all things nautical. The museum is crammed with ropes and brass bells, passenger ship memorabilia, port holes, fish nets, buoys, ship's timber and log books along with a host of other items they've rescued from the rubbish pile.

A museum of all things nautical

'We both love the water and we both love vessels, particularly wooden ones of course, but we also love putting things together again.'

This becomes ever more apparent as you wander around their riverside flotilla. Berthed next to their tugboat home, and across the park from the chart room, is their other passion, a floating Maritime Gallery and a monument to the efforts of these two bower birds. On the floating gallery, you'll find Chris' paintings along with those of other local artists.

In keeping with their passion, the Crabtrees have focused on nautical themes in the gallery, such as paintings of old paddlesteamers on the Murray, fishing fleets on the Spanish coast and the beauty of the Greek Islands. The gallery is housed in another labour of love, once unflatteringly known as Barge MTB-B-Six, a Second World War ammunition barge used in the invasion of Sicily. Judy and Chris found it at Port Adelaide, shipped it to Goolwa and began a lengthy restoration project.

At the Crabtree's gallery, nothing nautical goes to waste. The ceiling timbers are from the *Charles Sturt*, a famous vessel that was beyond restoration when Chris and Judy found it. During its heyday it played a key role in the construction of the Goolwa Barrages. Now the Captain Sturt contributes to an arts and maritime complex that draws a range of responses:

'People either say, You've got a wonderful lifestyle here, or they say, You're totally mad. The bank doesn't lend to you on anything that flies or floats, not that we've found anyway. It's something that we've wanted to do, we've done it and we love it. We're hoping to pass on our passion and we know that there will be people who will come here and say, Well, if they can do it, so can we.'

The Goolwa Maritime Gallery is open from Thursday to Sunday from 10 am until 4 pm. A short walk from the gallery is Hector's Shed, a old boat-building shed, also rescued by the Crabtrees, and crammed with memorabilia. Ask them to point the way.

Curson Place, Goolwa
South Australia 5214
Tel (08) 8555 3392
email crabtree@dove.net.au
website www.murray-river.net/
maritime-museum
Open Thursday to Sunday
10 am to 4 pm

Goolwa
Maritime
Gallery
(upstream
from the
Goolwa Wharf)

Kangaroo Island

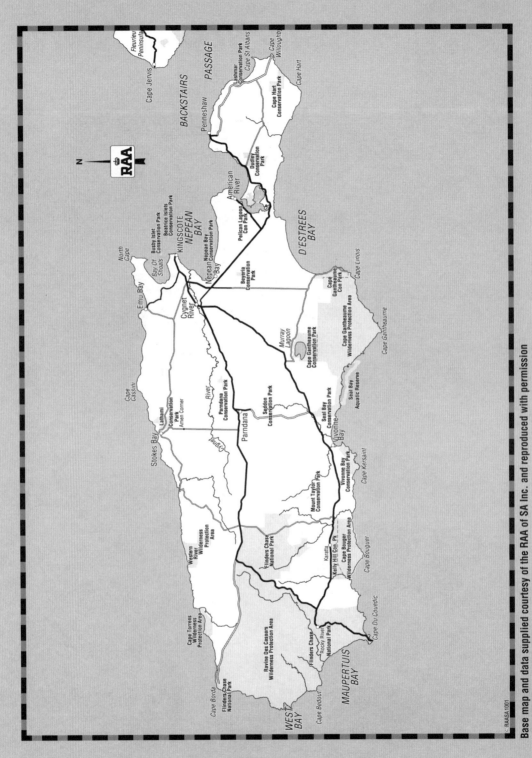

Reverse: Kangaroo Island kangaroo with joey   Photo by Pete Dobre

... enter a unique world where nature still holds her own.

North Coast, Kangaroo Island   Photo by Pete Dobre

From Munich to Modbury, Kangaroo Island is regarded as one of Australia's best nature holiday destinations. About 160,000 people including 40,000 from overseas visit the island each year, descending upon a mere four thousand or so Islanders. There is no bridge to Kangaroo Island; when you step off the ferry, you enter a unique world where nature still holds her own.

It's a big island, about 150 kilometres long, and about one-third of it is national park or conversation park. KI, as it's known locally, is a place without the environmental scourge of rabbits and foxes. There are no huge tourism resorts either. And that's because to get here you have to ferry Backstairs Passage, an ocean-filled trench cut from the tail end of the Mount Lofty Ranges by an ancient glacier a couple of ice ages back. The *Sealion 2000* ocean-going ferry spans the gap between Cape Jervis on the tip of the Fleurieu Peninsula and the holiday town of Penneshaw on the eastern end of Kangaroo Island. It's the main transport link for the islanders, their industries, and their visitors.

Tips From the Crew

- Jeff drives us everywhere and he recommends stocking up on supplies at Parndana in the centre of the island – it's the last place you can buy petrol if you're heading for Cape Borda.

- Jeff also recommends enjoying a walk on a deserted beach, kangaroo spotting at sunset, eating fish and chips on the beach as the sun goes down and making the most of the animal nightlife which he says is very special.

- Lisa says you must make time for a meal at the Cape Willoughby Lighthouse Cafe. The local food and wine is fantastic and the view over the cliffs at sunset is to die for. Be sure to book for this one.

- Trevor suggests having a yarn to the locals about their best fishing story. You'll be amazed at the ones that got away!

Seal Bay is among a mere handful
of accessible seal colonies anywhere in the world.

Andrew, Ron and Jeff at Cape du Couedic
Lighthouse   Photo by Andrew McEvoy

Many visitors catch the tour bus to the other end of the Island and Cape du Couedic. If you're collecting photographs on Kangaroo Island, there's one remote southern coast beach that has to be on your itinerary. Seal Bay Conservation Park is about an hour's drive from Kingscote and home to several hundred Australian sealions. It's a privilege to walk among one of a mere handful of accessible seal colonies anywhere in the world.

No trip to this natural paradise would be complete without spending time at the Flinders Chase National Park at Kangaroo Island's western end. Here you'll find crowds of kangaroos and wallabies to keep you company.

More than half of the population of Kangaroo Island live in Kingscote on the north coast and they're fiercely proud of their place in South Australian history. Months before the HMAS *Buffalo* sailed into Holdfast Bay several ships came to Reeves Point near modern Kingscote. As it turned out, water supply was a major problem and the pioneer settlement languished. But those who stayed on planted a mulberry tree in 1837, and it's still going strong today.

I Didn't Know That!

- Kelly Hill Caves in the south-west of the Island were first discovered in 1880 when a horse called Kate Kelly fell into a hole there.

- In 1947, one-third of Kangaroo Island was subdivided for the Soldier Settlement Scheme providing land for soldiers returning from the Second World War.

- Penneshaw used to be called Hog Bay because the French explorer Nicholas Baudin dropped off thirty pigs at this spot as food for future sailors.

- American River was named after the American sealers who lived here long before official settlement.

- Sealions at Seal Bay laze around on the beach because they've usually just spent three or fours days out at sea hunting for food!

In 1802 Matthew Flinders came ashore and killed thirty-one kangaroos for fresh meat. In gratitude, he called his landfall Kangaroo Island.

In March 1802 Matthew Flinders sheltered from a gale in the waters off the north coast of Kangaroo Island. His crew came ashore and killed thirty-one kangaroos for fresh meat. In gratitude he called his landfall Kanguroo Island, which was later changed to its present spelling. He also named the Backstairs Passage to the long gulfs of South Australia.

A couple of weeks later, Nicholas Baudin came past, just after the famous encounter of the two ships of warring nations that gave Encounter Bay its name. Baudin returned the next summer to name Kangaroo Island's south coast features after a winter break in Port Jackson, and Sydney Town. Having circled round to the northern side, his crew came ashore at Penneshaw for water and carved Frenchman's Rock. It is now safe in the Gateway Visitor Centre.

In the early 1800s, sealers and escaped convicts lived on Kangaroo Island. These rough-edged early residents brought Aboriginal women to the island from the mainland and Tasmania, often against their will. Carbon dating of stone tools and campsites in the early 1900s indicate that Aboriginal people have not lived on Kangaroo Island for at least ten thousand years.

The island definitely spells food, wine and wildlife these days and there's fabulous accommodation to suit all budgets. The *Postcards* crew roamed KI from top to bottom and picked out places that captured our hearts and tastebuds.

Tammar wallaby

Want More Information?

SA Visitor and Travel Centre
1300 655 276

The Gateway Visitor Information Centre
(08) 8553 1185

Kangaroo Island website
www.tourkangarooisland.com.au

Sealink website
www.sealink.com.au

National Parks and Wildlife SA
(08) 8553 2381

RAA Touring (maps and guides)
(08) 8205 4540

SA Tourism Commission website
www.southaustralia.com

***Postcards* website**
www.postcards.sa.com.au

Kangaroo Island Diving Safari
with Ron Kandelaars

A s we head out on Jim Thisleton's catamaran, the physical beauty of the north coast of Kangaroo Island looms large. Forces from long ago have pushed layers of sedimentary rock towards the heavens, resulting in a stunning, striped wall of cliffs that rise as high as 270 metres and offer the perfect backdrop for divers.

The Arches, where one secret chamber gives way to another

Jim guarantees that you will meet nature up close on his safari. Before long we watch, mesmerised, as a common dolphin rides the catamaran's shockwave. Soon a bottlenose dolphin joins in, riding the waves belly-up. Kangaroo Island's position at the entrance to Gulf St Vincent provides a unique set of environmental conditions and, as Jim explains, results in an abundance of marine life.

'You've got the high cliffs and good waters along this coastline. Three ocean currents meet in the area, east, west and south, plus the warm water out of the Gulf. All this gives the range and diversity under the water that's probably unparalleled in the world. There's so much here that we don't know about. We had a marine biologist here with us for two days. She took twenty-one specimens to the Museum. Nine of them turned out to be previously unknown to science.'

Soon we're heading into an area known as the Arches, where one secret chamber gives way to another and seals roll and flip through the calm waters, luxuriating in the sparkle of the midday sun: a magical opening to a show that only gets better as we dive down below.

On our first dive with Jim we enter an underwater chamber about fifteen metres deep. Jim tells us to roll over on our bellies and we find ourselves surrounded by playful, curious seals.

After this first, gentle dive, we head into deeper water in search of the rare leafy seadragon. These sea creatures are extremely difficult to spot because of their ability to blend into the surrounding seagrass. The loss of much of our seagrasses on the mainland now threatens this beautiful creature, but here on Kangaroo Island, under the shelter of the northern cliffs, their habitat remains intact. Like the seahorse, seadragons are able to change colour depending on age, diet, location and even their level of stress. New research shows they can travel hundreds of metres from their home base and thanks to a sophisticated navigational system they are able to return to exactly the same spot.

'They're only found in southern Australian waters, so for international divers and photographers it's a unique experience to come to this area.'

Today we are lucky enough to spy some of these tiny creatures, along with fearsome giant rays and extraordinary blue gropers. Although the leafy seadragon is one of the smallest and slowest creatures down here, it remains fascinating to the international diving community.

If you'd like a wonderful underwater experience or just the chance to explore the awesome coastline of Kangaroo Island, then hop on board a charter with Kangaroo Island Diving Safaris. Jim's a qualified diving instructor and will soon have you feeling confident in the water. If you don't want to dive you can still enjoy the comfort of his catamaran, *Wind Cheetah*.

Contact Jim and Josie Thisleton
Tel (08) 8559 3225
email kids@kin.net.au

Kangaroo Island
Diving Safari

Cape Forbin Retreat
with Ron Kandelaars

Cape Forbin is an idyllic retreat with stunning views of the rugged coastline, sea and sky

Many of us would like to find a holiday retreat on the edge of the world, far removed from the daily whirl. Graham Burnell found his on the rugged north coast of Kangaroo Island.

This idyllic spot can only be reached by private road through adjacent farmland. Only guests to Cape Forbin Retreat are given the map to this part of the island, the idea being that when you get here you'll be alone to enjoy stunning views of the rugged coastline, sea and sky.

From the cliff-top you can see Cape Borda in the distance, the north-western tip of the island and Cape Torrens. Down below is De Mole Beach, where the De Mole River meets its end. It's a photographer's paradise – the coastal scrub ventures right to the edge of the cliff. So does Graham, when he takes guests to Cape Forbin itself, for one of his nature walks.

At Cape Forbin, you can have the beach to yourself. Don't expect to see anyone else's footprints. For most of the year the beach remains intact, except in winter when wild storms wash much of it away.

Nature is constantly reshaping Kangaroo Island's north coast, whether it's from one winter to the next or around four hundred million years ago, when Australia was still part of Gondwanaland. Back then, geological uplifting and jilting heaved an ancient and compressed sea bed skyward. Today, in some places, it towers hundreds of metres above Investigator Strait.

Graham Burnell says that every morning at Cape Forbin brings a different view. Wherever you look, the cliffs are topped by a thick forest of casuarinas, the perfect habitat for the ubiquitous crimson rosella. Nearby, the casuarina makes way for the spikey yacca, and open land once used for sheep grazing is now a feeding ground for native kangaroos.

After a day of taking in the wildlife and rugged beauty of this spot, you can relax back at Cape Forbin Retreat, a luxurious getaway in a remote location. The only intrusion you can expect is the evening procession of tammar wallabies – thirty or forty of them – who are as regular as clockwork.

Graham explains that visitors to Cape Forbin are amazed at what they find here:

'They're absolutely blown away. There is so much wild fauna around them and they can be a part of it. There are not many places that are genuinely wild – where you can just sit and it all happens around you.'

Cape Forbin Retreat is on Kangaroo Island's north coast near the western end of the island, about an hour's drive from Pardana.

Contact Graham Burnell
Tel (08) 8559 3219
website www.capeforbinretreat.com.au

Cape Forbin
Retreat

A Smorgasbord of Kangaroo Island Produce

with Lisa McAskill

Betty McAdam's Hog Bay Apiary has fifteen sites scattered around the island

Hog Bay Apiary

Most days of the week you'll find Betty McAdam on one of the back roads of the north coast. She knows every dusty turn-off to every stand of sugar gum along this stretch of coastline.

For an apiarist, Kangaroo Island offers the perfect combination: a clean island environment, sugar gums in blossom and the famous Ligurian bee, which dates back to the days of the Roman Empire. Betty says there are at least fifteen references in Roman literature to people who kept bees, including evidence that the poet and philosopher Virgil was a beekeeper. And in the tradition of this great thinker, the beekeepers who came to Cape Dutton on Kangaroo Island in the 1880s displayed remarkable foresight:

They understood the problems that are caused by hybridising bees when you have two races of bees in the same area. You lose the characteristics that you've been breeding for over thousands of years. So, they convinced the South Australian government of the day that

Kangaroo Island should be set aside just for the Ligurian bee and now it's the oldest bee sanctuary in the world.'

Betty's Hog Bay Apiary has fifteen sites scattered around the island and she's been told that she looks like an alien as she collects honey dressed up in her white protective clothing. Despite the precautions, bee stings are a regular occurrence. But Betty never tires of harvesting one of the most natural foods available. Her honey is available at most outlets on Kangaroo Island, the Adelaide Central Market and Muggleton General Store in Hahndorf.

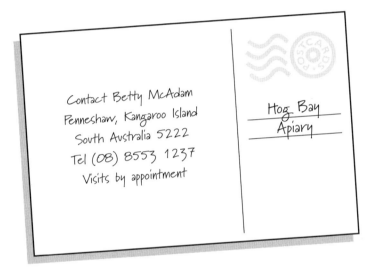

Contact Betty McAdam
Penneshaw, Kangaroo Island
South Australia 5222
Tel (08) 8553 1237
Visits by appointment

Hog Bay
Apiary

Dudley Partners Winery

Visitors to Kangaroo Island learn that the area around Penneshaw at the eastern end of the island is beautiful farming country. However, few know that it is also a wine-growing region, now officially recognised by the Geographical Indications Committee, the organisation that determines the boundaries of wine producing regions.

Here on the Dudley Peninsula the Dudley Partners Winery was created by three blokes who thought that making wine might be more interesting than farming wool and beef. They put in some vines and crushed their grapes by hand in the shearing shed. It resulted in a few hundred bottles of 'Shearing Shed Red'. The success of that vintage has led to expansion.

In 1999 and 2000 the partners produced 24,000 bottles each year and successfully exported their range to the United States. In 2001 they launched a new range and, despite a bad frost, produced 45,000 bottles including varietal chardonnay, cabernet sauvignon, shiraz – along with the ever-popular Shearing Shed Red for quaffing.

You'll find the winery on the Dudley Peninsula between Penneshaw and Cape Willoughby. Their cellar door is currently being renovated and re-opens for tastings in early 2002.

Dudley Peninsula
(between Penneshaw
and Cape Willoughby)
Tel (08) 8553 3298
or 0408 393 991
Cellar door re-opens for tastings
in early 2002

Dudley
Partners
Winery

Gum Creek Marron Farm

For Daniel Turner, a fourth-generation Kangaroo Island farmer, life on the land is all about adapting to change. He still runs sheep on his Cygnet River property just as his father did and his grandfather before him, but Daniel's move into aquaculture a decade ago is typical of the changes made by many Island farmers following a collapse in wool prices.

There are over one hundred registered marron growers on Kangaroo Island. While many of them sell wild marron harvested from creeks or rivers running through their properties, Daniel grows this freshwater crustacean in ponds. Starting with one pond many years ago, he's now dug one-hundred-and-twenty, and plans to more than double that number over an area of two hundred acres.

Daniel has cast the net far and wide in the search of the right ecological balance. He fills his ponds with goldfish to remove the algae, and trout to eat the aquatic insects that prey on juvenile marron. The marron are fed on a range of foods including wheat, barley, the occasional potato and pumpkin, lupin, and organic matter such as reeds and bark. At nearly forty dollars a kilogram, they're worth nurturing for both the domestic and export markets. Marron stay alive for twelve to fourteen days in a cool environment so they can be shipped fresh anywhere in the world.

The farm conducts hourly tours after midday and you can also grab a feed of marron or yabby at the cafe.

Gum Creek Road
(11 kilometres from Cygnet River)
South Australia
Tel (08) 8553 5255
Tours hourly after midday
Cafe open for lunch every day
(Friday, Sunday
and Monday in winter)

Gum Creek
Marron Farm

Farmhouse Cheeses

Kangaroo Island is rapidly carving out a niche on the national and international food circuit, with a number of small producers churning out award-winning products. Mos Howard at Farmhouse Cheeses near Penneshaw is one of them.

Each morning and afternoon you'll find him in the milking shed at the family property tending to a combined herd of Friesian and Aussie rèd cows.

After pasteurisation, Mos pours the milk into stainless steel vats at the nearby cheesery. He adds rennet to make it set, along with cheese cultures and mould spores. Next the curds are tipped into containers and left to the forces of time and gravity. After they've been drained and turned, they're placed in a saline solution that slowly absorbs into the cheese and forces out the whey.

Mos Howard, KI cheese-maker

At Farmhouse Cheeses they make brie and camembert – soft, moist cheeses that are quick to make. In fact, a brie or camembert from cow to consumer can take as little as two days, while a cheddar can take as long as twelve months.

Mos has always worked on the land but he finds cheese-making a lot easier and certainly cooler than his previous job working as a shearer, especially when he's in the cold room. Well, actually, he calls it 'the mould growing room':

'The mould creates a chemical reaction with the cheese curd, ripening it from the outside. That's why a young camembert or brie is runny at the edge but very firm in the middle.'

Mos says the best time to eat a brie is just before the use-by-date expires. And he should know. Farmhouse Cheeses won the champion Fancy Cheese at the Sydney Royal Show, the inaugural Australian Grand Dairy Award for White Mould cheese and Grand Champion cheese at the Australian Specialist Cheesemakers Association show.

The Farmhouse range is available at most outlets on Kangaroo Island, and major supermarkets and the Central Market in Adelaide.

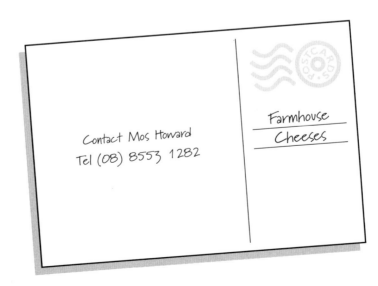

Contact Mos Howard
Tel (08) 8553 1282

Farmhouse
Cheeses

Kangaroo Island Olive Oil Company

There's an old saying in this business: vines are planted for your kids, olives for your grandchildren. But Dan and Sue Pattingale have planted their olives for themselves. They are the only olive oil producers on Kangaroo Island and they've set about establishing their dream at Stokes Bay on the North coast.

The Pattingales have been producing their own olive oil for years using wild olives collected from all over the Island. Sue says the fruit probably first made its way to Kangaroo Island more than a century ago, along with another Mediterranean import, the Ligurian bee. David and Sue have now planted two-and-a-half thousand trees and are harvesting commercial crops.

Vines are planted for your kids, olives for your grandchildren

For Dan, a former shearer, the trip to the olive oil mill is the culmination of both a career change and years of hope and hard work. At the press, the olives are washed and crushed, stones and all. The paste is warmed to thirty degrees and kneaded for up to an hour before being pumped into a large horizontal centrifuge. From there, the oil goes to a smaller separator for cleaning. Next, the oil is graded. Virgin olive oil is like fruit juice. It's simply squeezed from the fruit. Extra is the highest grade and Lampante, or lamp oil, is the lowest. Lampante needs to be refined, resulting in cheaper, mass produced olive oil.

Virgin olive oil production is taking place more and more throughout Australia along with the rush to plant trees. In the last three or four years at least five million olive trees have been planted in Australia. Over the years, there have been several attempts to grow commercial olive crops in South Australia. While the current demand for premium

Virgin olive oil is like fruit juice. It's simply squeezed from the fruit

olive oil has resulted in many new ventures, South Australia's Mediterranean climate has long provided a prime location for olive growing.

The Kangaroo Island Olive Oil Company took out the 1998 Champion Oil of the Show at the Sydney Royal Show and was runner-up in the 2000 South Australian Premier's Food and Fabric Award. You'll find their wares at the Adelaide Central Market and various outlets on Kangaroo Island.

Contact Dan and Sue Pattingale
Tel (08) 8559 2284
Available at the
Adelaide Central Market

Kangaroo Island
Olive Oil
Company

Cape du Couedic Lighthouse Cottages
with Ron Kandelaars

Each cottage at Cape du Couedic housed a lighthouse-keeper and his family   Photo by Andrew McEvoy

In the late nineteenth century, the only lighthouse on the hazardous west coast of Kangaroo Island was located at Cape Borda, now a part of the Flinders Chase National Park. Ships approaching the island further south from Cape Borda had to rely on navigation, and there were numerous shipwrecks and lives lost as a result. So, at the turn of the century, another lighthouse was built at Cape du Couedic.

Cape du Couedic is one of the most majestic spots on Kangaroo Island, and one of the loneliest. It took three years to build the jetty, storeroom, lighthouse and keepers' cottages, with the stone work taken from the nearby limestone cliffs.

It's not until you visit the place that you appreciate the courage and perseverance of families who worked and lived here. At times the isolation must have been unbearable. In the early days, food supplies arrived by boat every three months. Meat lasted just two weeks and, after that, people had to rely on their own catch of wild goats, wallabies and fish.

Rough seas added to the loneliness for these early residents as it was often difficult for supply ships to land, leaving the families waiting even longer for their fresh supplies. When it was safe for the ship to berth, the long-awaited cargo was offloaded at the end of the jetty, and the supplies were loaded into a basket attached to a flying fox and dragged up a channel cut into the cliff edge.

The lighthouse-keepers and their families lived in a shallow gully that offered shelter from the prevailing winds. The three cottages are named after the vessels that serviced the needs of the island: the *Troubridge*, the *Karatta* and the *Parndana*. Each housed a lighthouse-keeper and his family, with each keeper working an eight-hour shift.

Not surprisingly, the three families perched on a cliff, on what must have seemed like the edge of the world, occasionally got on each other's nerves. The general store was divided into three and each family was allocated a certain amount of food, so that – supposedly – there could be no quibbling about who got what.

Cabin fever, isolation and short supplies led to accusations about stolen food. One cantankerous lighthouse-keeper's wife was left dangling in the flying fox above Weirs Cove by members of another family, before being hoisted down the cliffs to a waiting supply ship.

If you'd like to find out more about the lighthouse families and stay in very reasonably priced accommodation, book into the Cape du Couedic lighthouse cottages. There are more cottages available for hire at the Cape Willoughby and Cape Borda lighthouses.

Contact Flinders Chase National Park
PMB 246, Kingscote
South Australia 5223
Tel (08) 8559 7235
Bring your own linen or hire it from
National Parks and Wildlife SA

Cape du
Couedic
Lighthouse
Cottages

The King's Fishing Charter
with Lisa McAskill

You've probably heard old fishermen say they remember the days when there were so many fish they almost jumped into the boat. Well, fish have become harder to come by these days. Perhaps that's why Kangaroo Island visitors call on Ian King, a professional fisherman who runs a charter operation out of American River. Ian reckons if the fish are there, he'll find them. And while they probably won't jump into the boat, he's got plenty of secrets locked away in his head that will put you ahead of the rest.

As we headed out into the bay, we took a slight diversion to visit an oyster farm run by A. Raptis & Sons, fish merchants and exporters. This type of farming is known as deep-sea aquaculture – an idea that Ian helped to get up and running in this area.

Ian King reckons if the fish are there, he'll find them

Although we would have loved to stop and test the oyster harvest, we had some serious fishing business of our own to get on with. Before long, we arrived in King George whiting territory and Ian insisted he could almost smell the fish as he shared his wisdom on how to bait the line:

'A bit of ground bait or berley helps to attract the fish, then hopefully take the bait on your hook. Drape the cockle on the hook, cast the line and take up the slack.'

Another successful King's fishing trip

If you feel like a fish out of water with a rod in your hand, a quick lesson from Ian will hook you in. It's all a matter of timing, and pretty soon we were on a roll. We fished into the sunset on the flat calm water in the bay at American River.

After catching about three dozen fat whiting we called it a day. You can't always guarantee that you'll catch a fish, but with a pro like Ian, the odds are in your favour. And even if you don't get a bite, it's hard to imagine a more relaxing way to spend a day.

Contact Ian and Margaret King
American River
South Australia 5221
Tel (08) 8553 7003
email thekings@kin.net.au

The King's
Fishing
Charter

Reverse: Sevenhill Winery   **Photo by Jeff Clayfield**

Base map and data supplied courtesy of the RAA of SA Inc. and reproduced with permission

In the mid-1800s, this was one of the world's truly multicultural settlements.

An easy drive from Adelaide to the Clare Valley reveals rolling hills, endless rows of grapevines, majestic Australian bushland and historic stone buildings. This country is home to premium wines, heritage accommodation and fabulous gourmet food.

The region's history is influenced by the Jesuits who, like many South Australian settlers of the 1800s, left their homeland to escape religious persecution. Originally from Austria, the Jesuits here established the Clare Valley's first winery in 1851, initially to make sacramental wines. Today you can visit their historic cellar door at Sevenhill and taste a wide range of wines, reflecting over one-hundred-and-fifty years of experience in South Australia.

There are more than thirty cellar doors dotted around the valley and they're all neighbours. Still, you'd be pushing it to visit them all in one day, so book into one of many luxurious bed and breakfast spots in the region.

On your way through from Adelaide, try a night at the Riverton Railway Station where you can stay in old train carriages or the Ladies' Waiting Room. The station has a wonderful gallery displaying local art including works by Robert Hannaford, who was commissioned to paint the official opening of

Keith at Sevenhill Winery

Photo by Jeff Clayfield

Tips From the Crew

- Ron suggests a drive in the Skilly Hills near Sevenhill. There are views across the vineyards, beautiful woodlands and cellar doors a plenty.

- Jeff says take a good pair of hiking boots with you and enjoy one of the many trails. His tip for budding photographers: use a wide-angle lens on your camera to capture the true sense of the landscape wherever you are.

- Trevor says Anlaby Station is his all-time favourite bed and breakfast location. He says there's literally a small village of houses on the property and it would make a perfect movie set.

- Lisa recommends Craigs Hill bed and breakfast at Clare, a one-hundred-year-old homestead set in thirty hectares of bushland.

- Keith says to look out for Kapunda's eight-metre high bronze statue 'Map Kernow' dedicated to the 1840s copper miners.

Vineyard Blues by Murray Edwards

Copyright Murray Edwards

parliament during the Centenary of Federation celebrations. At the Medika Gallery at Blyth you can grab a few tips from artist Ian Roberts, who paints beautiful watercolours of Australian wildlife. And make sure to visit Murray Edwards' mud-brick studio, Corella Hill at Watervale, and absorb his subtle impressions of the Clare Valley.

The Ngadjuri people inhabited this region before white settlement. They lived in the hills between Gawler and Orroroo for thousands of years before a deluge of migrants from all over the world descended on the Burra and Kapunda copper mines in search of work and wealth. Incredibly, in the mid 1800s, this was one of the world's truly multicultural settlements. Today you can grab a 'Passport key' in Burra and rediscover the enormous mines and the once bustling town.

The Clare Valley Riesling Trail along the old railway line links the wineries and small towns in the region and you can walk or ride your bike through the beautiful countryside. The views to Gulf St Vincent at the Spring Gully Conservation Park are definitely worth taking in. Spring Gully is just one of many stunning parks in this area, where you'll find gorges, forests, unspoilt wilderness and diverse wildlife.

At the southern end of the Clare Valley is the pretty, historic town of Auburn, filled with National Trust listed buildings, restaurants and heritage accommodation. The Mount Horrocks cellar door is now in the restored Railway Station there. The birthplace

 I Didn't Know That!

- Spalding is the largest water catchment area in South Australia and a great place to catch plenty of trout.

- Six hundred percent profit! That's what a syndicate of Adelaide businessmen made over four years on their capital investment in the Burra 'Monster Mine'.

- Martindale Hall, where *Picnic at Hanging Rock* was filmed, was built in 1879 by Edmund Bowman. There's a local myth that he built the grand home for his bride-to-be, but she jilted him. Today you can stay overnight there and experience life in a country manor, very much as the Mortlock pastoralist family left it.

- Thousands of trees were cut down in Burra's mining heyday to keep the fires burning, leaving the town's surrounding hills desolate. The success of the mine, however, saved the colony of South Australia from bankruptcy.

- Australia's first political assassination took place at the Riverton Railway Station in 1921.

of poet C.J. Dennis, Auburn celebrates its favourite son with an annual literary festival.

Another blessed spot in the Clare Valley is Mintaro, where time seems to stand still. Mintaro was settled in 1849 and you'll be charmed by its antiquated village. There are churches, shops, gardens, a nursery and even a garden maze. Have a beer and a pizza, cooked in an 1854 wood-fired oven, at the Magpie and Stump Hotel or try Devonshire tea at the Teapot Inn, home of the Mintaro Historical Society. Just out from Mintaro is a magnificent mansion, Martindale Hall, where you can stay in the manner to which you'd like to become accustomed.

Where General MacArthur stood and declared, 'I shall return'.

To the north of the valley you'll find the old railway town of Terowie, where United States General Douglas MacArthur stood and declared, 'I shall return,' during the Second World War after returning from the Philippines with defeat looming. Terowie was declared an historic township in 1985. In its Pioneer Gallery you can explore the town's past through a collection of photographs and archives.

The region is circled by farming land and townships, where families have worked the land for generations. Magnificent homesteads and stone buildings, each with a tall tale to tell, walking trails, coffee shops and the bucolic buzz, all make the farming areas delightful destinations.

Whether you're after rolling hills, rural history, a glass of cool, crisp riesling, a superb feast or a night tucked between luxurious sheets, you'll find it in the Clare Valley and Mid North, just a couple of hours from Adelaide.

Want More Information?

SA Visitor and Travel Centre
1300 655 276

Clare Valley Visitor Information Centre
1800 242 131

Clare Valley website
www.clarevalley.com.au

Clare Valley Wine Region Guide
1800 242 131

Burra Visitor Information Centre
(08) 8892 2154

Kapunda Visitor Information Centre
(08) 8566 2902

National Parks and Wildlife SA
(08) 8892 3025

RAA Touring (maps and guides)
(08) 8205 4540

SA Tourism Commission website
www.southaustralia.com

***Postcards* website**
www.postcards.sa.com.au

Eudunda — Colin Thiele Country
with Keith Conlon

The Sun on the Stubble and The Shadow on the Hills, two of Colin Thiele's books, come alive amongst the wheat paddocks and old stone barns of the Eudunda area. This is Colin Thiele country, and I carved a trail through historic Eudunda to pay tribute to one of Australia's best-loved storytellers.

The town that gave birth to the famous author is around one-hundred-and-thirty years old. Eudunda sits high in the ranges beyond the Barossa Valley, ninety minutes' drive from Adelaide.

For thousands of years, the Ngadjuri Aboriginal people called the gully above the town Eudunda-kawi, meaning water out of the ground. The spring fed a small creek, and early European stockmen watered their cattle here. Near where the single-storey colonial Eudunda Hotel stands today, an enterprising fellow called Henry Watson set up a grog shop in 1870, to water the horsemen. Within a couple of years, a pub was built and it wasn't long before Eudunda had all the trappings of a farming town.

The Ngadjuri people called the gully above Eudunda *kawi*, meaning water out of the ground

The land around the town attracted the same breed of hard-working Silesian settlers who founded Hahndorf, Lobethal and the Barossa Valley. Among these settlers was Colin Thiele's grandfather.

On a rambling dirt road, high on a long ridge, we found the family farm where Colin spent his boyhood. The cottage is set in wheat paddocks well back from the road, still surrounded by old stone outhouses and barns. In his first novel, Thiele wrote about 'the morning light, golden on the stubble', and continued:

'far up the slopes towards the range, the patches of fallow stretched rich and brown and the magpies were circling and carolling above the gums'.

On our visit, we marvelled at the beauty of his country – it was exactly as he described it.

A few kilometres south, Eudunda's early growth spurts have left their legacy in a well-preserved town. Good wheat years in the 1880s were followed by drought and depression, and the stoic cockies responded by forming a famous regional institution, the Eudunda Farmers Co-Op. It peaked at more than fifty shops around South Australia, and the town supermarket is still a part of it. In the main street there are still several shop signs that reflect the Germanic heritage of Eudunda. Colin Thiele, a revered educator as well an author, was born into this farming community in November 1920.

Only German was spoken on Colin's family farm, and he learned to speak and write English in a tiny school at Julia. His beloved teacher's wet-day storytelling sowed more of the seeds that would bloom into a fabulous career.

Speaking of stories, young Colin came to a pretty cottage in Eudunda to live with two eccentric bachelor uncles, Fred and August, for his upper primary years. Around the fire at night, they told ghost stories – so convincingly, as Thiele puts it in *Dew on My Boots*, that he usually went to bed in a state of shock.

The nineteenth-century Eudunda Mill remains a landmark on a bend between the old and deserted first shopping street and the town centre. It was the birthplace of the Laucke flour-milling tradition and the source of Mrs Thiele's farm supplies. The money from her cream sales, however, went to support her son's education.

In the old railway yards across the road the tall white silos fill up with the wheat harvest. Across from the now sadly dilapidated Eudunda railway station, Colin would watch the wheat-stacks 'rise up into the sky' each Christmas:

'with the centre … still a jumble of hollows, nooks and ridges – marvellous for races and Sunday games'.

A bronze sculpture of Colin Thiele and Mr Percival the pelican from *Stormboy*

The wheat stacks were a favourite nestling spot for lovers, too.

A few kilometres along the track, Colin Thiele caught the train every day at Hampden siding to go to high school; it was a half-hour bicycle ride in the dark along a rutted road to catch the seven am train, returning at eight-thirty at night to ride home. During those school and train-carriage hours, he read the classics and watched the undulating countryside go by, and buckets more seeds were sown.

Colin Thiele turned eighty in 2000, and the town gathered to celebrate around a bronze sculpture of their famous son, notebook in hand with Mr Percival, the pelican from *Stormboy*, at his side. This wonderful man and inspiring writer has been driven into exile in Queensland by ill health and arthritis, but you can be sure he's here in spirit. As he writes of his boyhood in Eudunda: 'you soak it up through your boot-soles'.

If you'd like to soak up some Eudunda spirit, contact the local tourism association. Many of Colin Thiele's books are available in major bookshops.

PO Box 1, Eudunda
South Australia 5374
Contact Peter Herriman
Tel (08) 8581 1958
email ecbat@websouth.com.au
website www.websouth.com.au/ecbat/

Eudunda
Community
Business and
Tourism
Association

Some of Colin Thiele's books include:
The Sun on the Stubble (1961), The Shadow on the Hills (1977),
Storm Boy (1963), Blue Fin (1969)

The Riesling Trail
with Lisa McAskill

The Clare Valley is classic wine country with scenery as satisfying as its flavours. The Riesling Trail has been built so that visitors can experience the valley from end to end. It offers twenty-seven kilometres of cycling and walking tracks that weave their way through this enchanted part of South Australia.

The trail began with a group of local winemakers who saw the potential for the disused railway line from Riverton to Spalding that ran through their region. The railway workers had already done the hard work for them by clearing and levelling the land for the tracks. It was an obvious trail along a skinny nature reserve.

The railway service to Clare began in 1918, after decades of argument. By the 1980s, Australian National was looking for an excuse to close it, and that came with the savage Ash Wednesday bushfires of 1983. The fires damaged sleepers and services along the single track. The track was eventually demolished at greater expense than its estimated cost of repair and the old tracks were sent up to a train line in Bundaberg, Queensland.

The Jesuits established the Clare Valley's first winery, Sevenhill, in 1851   Photo by Jeff Clayfield

The loss of the railway has been the cyclist's and hiker's gain, and the locals decided to name the trail after the Clare Valley's much celebrated grape. About seven kilometres south of Clare, you'll find a quaint feature of the trail, a lightweight replica of an old rail bridge that spans the old quarry road. Several wineries are also creating picnic locations along the way so that you can take time out to explore the sights.

The oldest vine plantings in the area are at Sevenhill, where Austrian Jesuits planted vines in 1851 and began making wine. The wine was used during worship and supplied churches across Australia and other parts of the southern hemisphere. Sevenhill Cellars still supplies much altar wine but also sells regional reds and whites via its cellar door.

The old railway line snakes from one side of the valley to the other, sometimes revealing sprawling vistas of wheat paddocks and vineyards. There are more than thirty bed and breakfast cottages, and several hotels, motels and caravan parks in the area, so you might well find that your single day's ride turns into an epic trek – especially if you're tempted by the fruits of the vine on offer all around.

The Riesling Trail ends at Auburn's old railway station. A few years ago, the government sold the 1916 station, and it's now been beautifully restored as the cellar door for Mt Horrocks Wines.

To get on the Riesling Trail all you have to do is pick up a brochure from the Clare Tourism Office or the Department of Recreation and Sport. It has a map of the trail and includes information on car parks and bike hire.

Department of Recreation and Sport
Tel (08) 8416 6677

Clare Valley Visitor
Information Centre,
Old Town Hall, Clare
South Australia 5453
tel (08) 8842 2131
Open every day.

The
Riesling Trail

Bundaleer Forest

with Keith Conlon

In autumn, the yellows, golds and reds in the soft sunlight could be mistaken for some of the old gardens in the Adelaide Hills. But the magnificent century-old oaks, elms and other European species that turn on a show each year are instead found on the slopes of historic Bundaleer Forest in South Australia's Mid North.

Curnow's Hut is now an overnight rest-stop for hikers and bike-riders   Photo by Andrew McEvoy

These trees were planted in Australia's first commercial forest from 1876, as part of a state timber industry experiment to find a suitable plantation tree.

These forestry pioneers eventually settled on a Californian pine, and so *Pinus Radiata* is one of the main softwood timbers grown in South Australia today. Plantings extend over about half the forest reserve at Bundaleer. That leaves open, rocky, grassed ridges, and creeks and hillsides that are now mapped out on walking trails, fanning out from a sports ground and shaded picnic ground.

Bundaleer Forest is about 200 kilometres north of Adelaide, or about a two-and-a-half hour car journey via the Clare Valley. It is near a picturesque agricultural town, Jamestown, which invites townsfolk and visitors to picnic on the Belalie Creek under giant redgums planted by its first mayor, Dr J. Cockburn. His bust is a feature of the extraordinarily wide main shopping street, and the local population of 2000 or so is justifiably proud of the mayor who went on to become a premier of South Australia, and a strong advocate of Federation.

Bundaleer Forest has been used as a spectacular venue for world-class events, with performances by visiting musicians, poets and artists. These events are combined

Oaks, elms and other European species were first planted in Bundaleer Forest in 1876   Photo by Keith Conlon

with guided trail walks that highlight the forest's unique place in history. The Conservator's Hut, found along the trail, is flanked by huge gums and poplars, and was home to the first Conservator of Forests in South Australia. John Ednie Brown, a Scot, was more than an internationally experienced forester, he was a nineteenth-century Trees For Life type, advocating tree-planting everywhere.

A few kilometres away in the reserve, along a valley road dotted with farm cottage ruins and home orchards, is Curnow's Hut. Great gums and exotics frame the old stone cottage that once housed history-making nurseryman William Curnow, who used cut bamboo to nurture his seedlings – an idea that eventually evolved into the black-plastic tubes we buy our seedlings in today. Curnow's Hut is now an overnight rest stop for hikers and bike-riders making their way along the Heysen and Mawson Trails that snake through the forest.

So, head up to Bundaleer Forest. It's a wonderful opportunity to meander through the picturesque hills and dales of South Australia's Mid North.

Forestry SA Wirrabara Office
Tel (08) 8668 4163

Jamestown Caravan Park
Tel (08) 8664 0077

Bundaleer
Forest

Redruth Gaol

with Ron Kandelaars

urra is a well-heeled heritage town that retains ample evidence of the wealth generated in the 1860s and 1870s at one of the largest mining operations in the world. Back then, tales of miners earning up to five guineas per week reached far and wide, resulting in a flood of treasure hunters and drifters to the Mid North town.

Without a police force or resident magistrate to enforce the law, Burra's drinking rate rose as rapidly as the population. Sly grog shops were a feature of what became Australia's largest inland town at the time. Until 1880 the legal minimum drinking age in the colony was just twelve, and hotel opening hours stretched from five in the morning until eleven at night. Bustling Burra developed a fearsome reputation, with 'the drink' the most common cause of crime during the life of the mine. Pretty soon, perpetrators were taking a spell 'at Her Majesty's pleasure' in the Redruth Gaol.

Redruth Gaol was built to last in 1856

Redruth was built to last in 1856. It cost the government more than £3000 and was the first country gaol in the colony. For its thirty male and female inmates, housed in adjoining yards, this was a loathsome place. Redruth was known as 'Perry's Hotel' after the first jailer Thomas Perry.

Unlike the inmates, Perry was lucky enough to have a view to the paddocks beyond. Redruth Gaol was set back from the mine and the town, well outside any possible mining claims. The fact that it was nicknamed a 'hotel' reflects the ironic humour which the hardened Cornish miners brought to this part of the state. There certainly would have been little warmth within the gaol walls in winter, with low temperatures, occasional snowfall and stark living conditions.

The building closed as a jail in 1894 and for a short time was home to the Wollacott family. It opened three years later as the Redruth Girls Reformatory. Thirty girls – the 'incorrigibles' from other institutions in Adelaide – were sent up here and they certainly made their presence felt, attempting a number of escapes. In 1922 the recalcitrant girls caused a riot and the government finally decided that 'stone walls a jail does not make'!

But it did make the perfect backdrop for some of the scenes in the South Australian Film Corporation's 1979 film *Breaker Morant*. Now the former gaol, private residence, reformatory and film set is open to everyone as part of the Burra Passport Key Trail. So come along and experience life on the inside. You can pick up a key at the town's visitor centre.

Passport Key available
from the Burra Visitor Centre
2 Market Square, Burra
South Australia 5417
Tel (08) 8892 2154
website www.weblogic.com.au/burra/

Redruth
Gaol

Murray Edwards' Corella Hill Studio
with Lisa McAskill

Murray Edwards' Corella Hill Studio, perched on a hill at Watervale, offers the perfect inspiration for a painter: sweeping views of vineyards and the ever-changing light of the Clare Valley. Murray paints in the impressionist style and he says his work is more involved with concepts and moods than with realism:

'The sun is starting to come out from behind that cloud now. You can see it moving across the vines. That's part of what you try to capture, a brief moment, and then it's gone again.'

In these brief moments, Murray Edwards has captured much of the Clare Valley including the vineyards at Sevenhill. The artist scours the region for ideas, with every bend or rise providing yet another possibility. Murray sees each canvas as a frenzied race against time and the light as he strives to capture what he sees:

'I once watched the sun break through and reflect the clouds onto a wet road. It was purple, and there was no other colour I could paint it. That's why I am inspired by Van Gogh. He had the courage to paint what he saw rather than what the market wanted.'

Corella Hill is a mud-brick studio, set on a thirty-eight acre ridgetop. Murray says an artist can get lazy though, tucked away in a hillside retreat, so he regularly travels to the vastness of the Mid North where the painter is small, and the subject is big:

'I feel infinitesimal when I'm there – like a dot in the landscape. That doesn't bother me because the size of the landscape sets me free. There are endless possibilities out there: beauty, freedom, all those sorts of things.'

For this former teacher the move to life as a financially insecure artist was gradual, but inevitable. The death of his inspirational father after a long battle with cancer caused Murray to reassess his life:

Corella Hill Studio offers sweeping views of vineyards and the ever-changing light of the Clare Valley

'I think death invites you to take a look at your values. Is it important to stick to your job until the gold watch comes or is it more important to do what you feel is really you? People come up here and I can see the cogs turning around in their heads. Then I know that they've got something else from their visit apart from looking at pictures or talking to an artist.'

If you're in need of inspiration, visit Murray in his Corella Hill Studio from Thursday to Sunday. It's on the road to Olssen Wines. Follow the signs from Watervale.

Watervale
South Australia 5452
Tel (08) 8843 0036
Open Thursday to Sunday.
Other times by appointment.

Murray
Edwards'
Corella Hill
Studio

Map labels:
Stockwell
HWY
GREENOCK
A20
STURT
Light Pass
River
Nuriootpa
Marananga
WAY
Seppeltsfield
Penrice
Para
Angaston
VALLEY
TANUNDA
B19
Bethany
North
BAROSSA
Rowland Flat
Mt Crawford Forest
Kaiser Stuhl Con. Pk
N
RAA
Mountadam Vineyard
Eden Valley

Reverse: Barossa Valley vineyards   Photo by Doug Coats

The heritage town of Gawler, around forty kilometres from Adelaide, is the traditional gateway to the wine and food lover's Elysian fields. Early European pioneers passed through Gawler before settling in the region now known as the Barossa Valley. Early Gawler was an engineering and locomotive building centre and home to many intellectuals and lovers of art. Today it is a pretty place to stop in order to explore many beautiful stone buildings and houses that take you back to an era of grace. Gawler boasts that the 'Song of Australia' was first played in its fine Institute.

A defining self-sufficient approach to life — including a wonderful range of preserved food.

In 1836 mineralogist Johannes Menge was sent by the South Australian Company to survey the ranges north of Adelaide. Menge's report was positive in spades and his

prediction of future vineyards in the 'New Silesia' has proved correct. The first German-speaking migrants arrived in the Barrosa (its original name until it was misspelt on a map) in 1842 and established the town of Bethany, near where English free settlers had arrived two years earlier. German-speaking settlers continued to arrive in the area along with the English who mostly preferred the town of Angaston as their home. The talents, cultures and heritage of both groups

Kaiser Stuhl Conservation Park

Photo by Bernd Stoecker

Tips From the Crew

- Mike says to look out for wedge-tailed eagles and parrots at the Kaiser Stuhl Conservation Park.

- Lisa loves to drop into Maggie Beer's Farm Shop at Nuriootpa for some of her legendary treats. You can also have a coffee or a glass of wine there.

- 'King of the Kids' Ron recommends taking the brood to see 'Norm's Coolies', a performing sheep dog show at Tanunda.

- Keith reckons Linke's Central Meat Store in Nuriootpa is fantastic – especially the Barossa mettwurst.

- Jeff says wherever you go you should always pack a camera, binoculars, walking shoes, shorts and detailed road maps (a four-wheel-drive vehicle is an optional extra). His other golden rules are: enjoy sunsets and sunrises, talk to the locals, eat local produce, stay overnight and do lots of walking.

helped to set up a region with a strong, religious work ethic, an artistic flavour and a defining self-sufficient approach to life – including a wonderful range of food.

Barossa wines are in demand across the globe. The industry has been nurtured and developed over the past one-hundred-and-fifty years into an expert craft. Originally financed by wealthy English free settlers in the 1850s and 1860s, today more than five hundred vignerons ply their trade in the region. The industry was established on a world scale by names like Gramp, Seppelt, Lehmann, Blass and Hill-Smith, and today the

'boutique' wineries have forged reputations as quality wine producers also. The Barossa Wine Centre in Tanunda has a wealth of information on the wineries, along with the history and culture of the region.

There's an exceptional food culture present in the Barossa Valley. From the smoky butcher shops to the undeniable call of fresh crusty bread, make your way around and discover the many cheeses, olives, yabbies, German cakes, dried fruits, stone fruit, pickles, preserves and jams available. You might even get to taste traditional recipes that have been handed down through generations, often adapted to impart their own Barossa flavour.

Fabulous Barossa Valley food

I Didn't Know That!

- The Barossa Valley is just twenty kilometres long and fourteen kilometres wide but it's the largest single wine processing region in Australia.

- The 'Hoffnungsthal' site near Williamstown was once a village until it was destroyed by floods in 1853.

- The 'giant' Barossa wineries each crush over 10,000 tonnes of grapes each year.

- Misspellings have crept in over the years: Colonel William Light originally named the Barrosa (now Barossa), the town of Lynedoch is now Lyndoch and the Greenoch Range became Greenock.

- Some Barossa vignerons use gnarled old shiraz vines, well over a century old, for wine production.

Whisper to each other down the one-hundred-and-forty-metre wall with its puzzling acoustics.

There are a number of parks, forests and walking trails to explore along the way. Take the family to the Whispering Wall at Cockatoo Valley and whisper to each other across the one-hundred-and-forty-metre wall with its puzzling acoustics. There are goldfields nearby, along with the beautiful bushland of Para Wirra Park. You can wander among fifty varieties of lavender at the Lyndoch Lavender Farm or lose yourself in the magnificent Mount Crawford Forest near Williamstown.

You can catch a fantastic view across the Valley from Mengler Hill Lookout at Tanunda, and the historic walks around this pioneering town let you glance into the region's past. At Tanunda you'll discover churches with exquisite stained-glass and ornate features while in nearby Bethany, the valley's original Lutheran settlement, you can walk around a village laid out in traditional Silesian style.

The Barossa Valley is crammed with amazing treats. You can get there by driving, taking a tour, or by climbing aboard one of the 1952 Bluebird carriages of the Barossa Wine Train: enjoy the journey, glass of wine in hand, as you gaze out at the view. *In vino veritas* indeed, but there are further treats in store for you as well. Do as the locals do, and allow plenty of time to take in what the Barossa has to offer.

Keith in the Barossa Valley

Want More Information?

SA Visitor and Travel Centre
1300 655 276

Barossa Wine and Visitor Centre
66–68 Murray Street, Tanunda
1300 852 982

Barossa Valley website
www.barossa-region.org

Barossa Wine Train
(08) 8212 7888

Gawler Visitor Centre
(08) 8522 6814

National Parks and Wildlife SA
(08) 8280 7048

RAA Touring (maps and guides)
(08) 8205 4540

SA Tourism Commission website
www.southaustralia.com

***Postcards* website**
www.postcards.sa.com.au

Luhrs Cottage
with Lisa McAskill

Luhrs Cottage is a reminder of how tough life was for the German pioneers   Photo by Eric Algra

Tucked away in the vineyards between Nuriootpa and Angaston is the tiny town of Light Pass. German-speaking settlers took up land in this area in 1845 and, not long after that, Johann Heinrich Luhrs accepted a call to teach at the new Lutheran school.

Johann built his four-roomed cottage around 1846, as a family home for him and his new wife, Anna, constructing the dwelling out of mud and straw around a hand-cut red-gum frame. The cottage was restored in 1984 and furnished with articles from the days when the Luhr family lived here.

Luhrs Cottage is a reminder of how tough life was for the German pioneers. Anna gave birth to the couple's six children in this cottage, one of them stillborn. Inside the home the woman was the head of the family, but with this role came a mountain of work. She had to help her husband in the fields, care for her family, grow vegetables, milk the cows, make the clothes, wash, mend and iron – and make her own candles and soap. And always, it must have seemed, Anna was pregnant with her next child.

Behind the cottage is a room that was built a few years later. It has been used as a bedroom, a Sunday School and for church guild meetings, but now it's dedicated to the old school days, with many original German books and wordcards on display. Until the advent of the First World War, German was often the only language taught in the Barossa Valley.

Luhrs Cottage offers you a glimpse into the early hard-working days of South Australia's German settlement, which has contributed so much to the state's vitality.

Light Pass Road,
Light Pass
South Australia
Open weekdays 9.30 am to 3.30 pm
and weekends 10 am to 4 pm

Luhrs
Cottage

Jacob's Creek

with Keith Conlon

I t's Australia's most famous creek. It certainly is in the United Kingdom, and probably in many of the fifty countries where the Jacob's Creek wine brand is sold. Some international drinkers think Jacob's Creek is a whole wine region, and that's understandable – it is the nation's biggest selling label. About one million glasses of it are drunk every day.

In fact, Jacob's Creek is only a few kilometres long, emerging out of the Barossa Range near its peak, Kaiser Stuhl, and gurgling along the river-red-gum-lined bed to the North Para River. The creek is bone dry at vintage time in autumn – yet the Jacob's Creek name conjures up an Amazonian flow of Australian 'sunshine-in-a-bottle'.

It all began one-hundred-and-fifty years ago just where the creek spills alluvial soil out of the hills. Here the first commercial vintage of Barossa wine was released in 1850 from a modest cellar and now-restored cottage.

The cottage was built by Johann Gramp, a young Bavarian banker who came to South Australia in the first year of the colony. A decade later, he came to Langmeil in the Barossa Valley, and bought land and planted vines on this spot. Today Orlando Wyndham have replanted his pioneering vineyard.

Back in 1850, Johann's first release was one small barrel – an octave – making about seven-dozen bottles. Today, over three-and-a-half million cases are exported to international markets. Orlando Wyndham has cleaned up the olive trees and fig thickets, and Jacob's, a classic Aussie creek again, befits its celebrated label. After all it's famous. Busloads of Brits insist on standing by the small creek sign on the main road to Tanunda to get a snapshot.

The man who gave the creek its name was none other than an assistant surveyor to Colonel William Light. Young William Jacob was aboard the *Rapid* as Light sought a site for the new city. Jacob surveyed the land around the creek in 1839, and within a year he made the area his home. With brother John and sister Ann, he built a homestead

Opposite: Jacob's Creek emerges out of the Barossa Range near its peak, Kaiser Stuhl Photo by Keith Conlon

overlooking the flood plain of his creek. Jacob also ran an early winery here, and the old Moorooroo cellar is now part of the classy Grant Burge Wines cellar-door operation.

There's a yarn that a couple of international tourists hopped into a cab at Adelaide Airport and said, 'Take us to Jacob's Creek!' The driver, we trust, also dropped in to Orlando Wyndham's cellar door in the old schoolhouse at Rowland Flat. During our short visit, German and English accents abounded. And that's where most of the Jacob's Creek label ends up: eight out of every ten bottles are exported.

Meanwhile, back in the creek itself, I was on a pilgrimage of sorts. Having known for years about 'Menge's Cave', I was keen to discover if this fabled spot was still visible. And there, close to Jacob's Creek's final gurgle, the legendary figure's home came into view. Johannes Menge was an energetic and eccentric mineralogist who became known as the 'Father of Mineralogy' in this state. There's substance in the claim that he is the 'Father of the Barossa' too, because he described the area as 'the cream, all the cream and nothing but the cream', commending it as vineyard country. This helped persuade the Klemzig Lutherans to set up the first villages in the Barossa Valley in 1842. Menge's half-house-half-cave location is not yet open to the public, but a new Jacob's Creek Visitor Centre is soon to be constructed close by.

Meanwhile, you can taste the famous drop at the Orlando Wyndham cellar door. If you're after a snapshot, look for a small sign marking the creek on the main road to Tanunda.

Barossa Valley Way, Rowland Flat
South Australia 5352
Tel (08) 8521 3140
Open 10 am—5 am weekdays,
10 am—4 am weekends
and public holidays

Orlando
Wyndham
Cellar Door

Barossa Valley Way, Tanunda
South Australia 5352
Tel (08) 8563 3700
Open every day 10 am—5 pm

Grant Burge
Cellar Door

Peter Carrigy, Wood Sculptor
with Ron Kandelaars

The gnarled features of fallen gum trees moulded by the wind and weather in a paddock in the Eden Valley provide inspiration for Peter Carrigy. At the Mountadam Winery he scours old woodpiles for raw material that he will eventually carve into beautiful pieces of art. This wood sculptor sees possibilities that are hidden from most eyes and soon part of the Eden Valley woodpile will probably find its way into a gallery. Peter describes his work as spiritual:

'I always say that trees are a link between the earth and the sky. I feel that I am tapping into the tree's energy. There's a phrase that's used quite often, that it is the soul of the tree.'

Mountadam Winery was established by the late winemaker David Wynn, son of a Polish immigrant with a love of the arts and a passion for woodcarving. A decade ago David saw Peter's early works, stock pieces like paperknives and platters, and urged him to branch out into the classic sculptures that have earned him commissions here and overseas:

'I think David was a kindred spirit and I believe that he was a frustrated artist. So it's almost like carrying on his vision.'

As part of that vision, the old woodpiles have been left as a habitat for local wildlife and for Peter Carrigy to rummage through. This is a far cry from early attitudes to our natural heritage.

'In the past, magnificent gum trees were seen as a pest, something to be cleared to make way for sheep or crops, or vineyards for that matter. In the early days we really didn't see timber like this as suitable for making furniture and so much of it ended up in fence posts or went up in smoke.'

Fallen gum trees in an Eden Valley paddock provide inspiration for wood sculptor Peter Carrigy

Now some of the remnants of our fallen past find their way to a back shed in suburban Adelaide Maylands and later to exhibitions overseas including a prestigious art fair in Chicago. Peter bases his sculptures on the Australian landscape, and is inspired by places he visits, like the Bungle Bungle Ranges in Western Australia's Kimberleys and South Australia's own Flinders Ranges. As he works, he describes one of his sculptures:

'I've been working this red gum to reflect a massive rockface, almost like clay, using wet and dry techniques, rubbing ochre into it and colour – yellow and orange.'

If you've seen the steep ridges of the Flinders Ranges from the air, you'll get a sense of what Peter is striving for, whether he's sculpting a piece for a company boardroom, or something more accessible for the home. His work is on show at the Jam Factory's city shop.

The Jam Factory
19 Morphett Street, Adelaide
South Australia 5000
Tel (08) 8410 0727
Open Monday to Friday
9 am–5.30 am,
weekends 10 am–5.30 pm

Peter Carrigy
Tel (08) 8363 1979

High Eden Road, Eden Valley
South Australia 5235
Tel (08) 8564 1101
Open every day 11 am–4 pm, except
Good Friday and Christmas Day

Mountadam
Vineyard
Cellar Door

Seasons of the Valley Cafe and Gallery
with Ron Kandelaars

The Barossa Valley was named by Colonel William Light after the Battle of Barrosa, fought in the Spanish Peninsula War in 1811. For many, it's now an ideal holiday retreat at any time of the year. And the shots taken by Angaston photographer Doug Coats that grace the walls of the Seasons of the Valley Cafe highlight the many faces of this magical valley.

You'll find fresh local produce along with photographs of the Barossa Valley in all its glory at Seasons of the Valley   Photo by Doug Coats

A few years back Doug and his wife, Marjorie, purchased Franklin House, the 1840s home of Angaston's first doctor, Horace Dean. 'Doctor' Dean went on to become a Legislative Councillor until he was forced to leave in disgrace when his medical degree was found to be a sham.

But here at the Seasons of the Valley, what you see is what you get: fresh cafe-style food made from local seasonal produce. Take Marjorie's home-made pasta for instance. She uses six cups of durum semolina and eight free-range duck eggs, and that's it. Let Marjorie mix them up and the result is delicious. The pasta is blanched in boiling water and ready in seconds. Fresh as you can get.

For Marjorie, this venture is just part of a thirty-year love affair with food. After years creating recipes for food companies and advertising magazines, she decided to go into the restaurant industry. While she was developing recipes Marjorie met Doug, who had the job of photographing her creations. Well, as the saying goes, they just 'clicked'.

Marjorie's passion is fresh food and that's why all the ingredients for her sauces come from the back yard. A combination of produce from the vegie patch and the home-made pasta machine is soon on your plate and, as you tuck in, you can also savour other seasonal produce: Doug's photographs of the ever-changing Barossa Valley in all its glory.

For a serving of fresh Barossa produce (including home-made ice-cream) and the local sights, head to the Seasons of the Valley Cafe and Gallery at Angaston.

6–8 Washington Street, Angaston
South Australia 5353
Tel (08) 8564 3688
Open daily from 10 am to 5 pm

Seasons of the
Valley Cafe
and Gallery

Butcher, Baker, Winemaker Trail
with Keith Conlon

For a couple of months each autumn, thousands of people in our famous Barossa Valley get caught up in the crazy but crucial round-the-clock mayhem called vintage. I took the chance to sample the valley's colour and flavours using the new year-round Butcher, Baker, Winemaker Trail as a guide.

The Trail brochure lists about a dozen of the region's fifty or so wineries that feature local produce. It guided us to our first titillating taste, up the hill above the small Marananga settlement to the tiny Gnadenfrei Winery. Gnadenfrei's labels sit on premium wineshop shelves in New York and Boston, and it sells out at its cellar door in the first half of each year. Malcolm Seppelt, of the well-known winemaking dynasty, found his niche at Gnadenfrei two decades back, making a distinct western Barossa drop. His forebear Joseph Seppelt started the superb heritage winery at Seppeltsfield one-hundred-and-fifty years ago, and it has a well earned place on the trail. Joylene Seppelt, at Gnadenfrei, is on the trail too. She's a legend in her own lunchtime, choosing local produce to fill her splendid 'takeaway' picnic baskets. When the legendary Barossa brass bands play together under one giant tin roof during the Barossa Vintage Festival, Joylene lovingly prepares all the supper baskets.

The small, strung-out village of Bethany is where the Barossa Valley as we know it began back in 1842. Up the top of the Bethany Road, the quarry that provided the village church stone resonates with the slosh and grind of vintage. The Schrapel family have been growing grapes on the slopes of the range since the 1850s, and this generation has built a winery and a reputation that has put it on the international wine map. Visit the Bethany Wines cellar door and grab a couple of bottles of their delectable Pear Tree Cottage condiments.

While you're in the Barossa, you can't help but notice that each town has its own distinct flavour. Nuriootpa, for instance, enjoys the smoky aroma and flavours of

Linke's Meat Store. I joined Graham Linke in his customised smokehouse behind the shop, and it was, well, very smoky. As he raked the burning wood coals, he told me about the weekly cycle of mettwursts, chickens, the delectable eye fillet of pork – lachsschinken – and the bacon.

The Barossa is a yeast-lover's paradise

If the butchers are a must on the Trail, so are the bakers. Tanunda is home to a yeast-lover's paradise, the Apex Bakery. The Fechners use traditional recipes and an oven that go back to the 1920s. Another town, Angaston, boasts the best baguettes on the Trail – you'll find them at Angaston Gourmet Foods. Just out of town, the oldest family winery in Australia, Yalumba, waves the Barossa flag around the world, displaying its distinctive clock tower on its labels. During the Vintage Festival after Easter, a quiet lawn behind the old cellars at Yalumba is transformed into a two-day Harvest Market where visitors flock to peck at their delicious regional produce.

The Butcher, Baker, Winemaker Trail is all about bringing the district together to show a unique food and wine culture that has been around for the past one-hundred-and-sixty years. Pick up a copy of the brochure and make sure you set off with an empty stomach.

Butcher, Baker, Winemaker Trail brochures available from the Barossa Wine and Visitor Centre.

66 Murray Street, Tanunda
South Australia 5253
Tel 1800 812 662
website www.barossa-region.org
Open Monday to Friday 9 am–5 pm,
weekends 10 am–4 pm

Barossa Wine
and Visitor
Centre

Yorke Peninsula

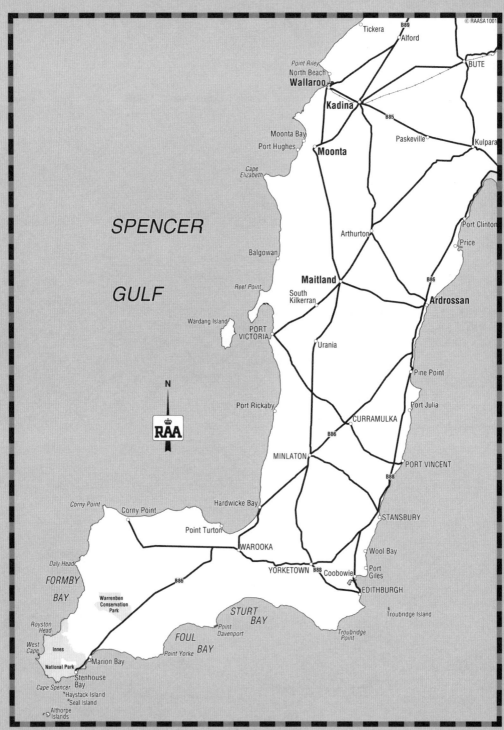

© RAASA 1001

Tickera   **B89**
Alford
BUTE
Point Riley
North Beach
Wallaroo
Kadina
    B85
Moonta Bay
Port Hughes
Paskeville
Kulpara
Moonta
Cape
Elizabeth

SPENCER

Port Clinton
Price
Arthurton

Balgowan

GULF

B86
Reef Point
Maitland
South
Kilkerran
Ardrossan

Wardang Island
**PORT
VICTORIA**
Urania

Pine Point

N

Port Rickaby
Port Julia
RAA

CURRAMULKA

B86
Port Vincent → **PORT VINCENT**
MINLATON
B88

Corny Point
Corny Point
Hardwicke Bay
STANSBURY

Point Turton

Wool Bay
WAROOKA
Daly Head

FORMBY
YORKETOWN **B88** Coobowie
Port
Giles
BAY
Warrenben
Conservation
Park
B86
STURT
BAY
EDITHBURGH
Royston
Head
Point
Davenport
Troubridge Island
West
Cape
Innes
FOUL
Troubridge
Point
Point Yorke *BAY*
National Park
Marion Bay
Stenhouse
Bay
Cape Spencer
Haystack Island
Seal Island
Althorpe
Islands

Base map and data supplied courtesy of the RAA of SA Inc. and reproduced with permission

Reverse: Innes National Park   **Photo by Bernd Stoecker**

Trevor, Andrew and Ron with Innes National Park ranger Richard Thomas (right)   Photo by Andrew McEvoy

How long 'til we get there?

For many South Australians travelling to 'Yorkes' evokes memories of caravan parks and shacks, fishing, swimming, surfing, crabbing and camping, exploring old mines and shipwrecks, checking the fishing buckets along the jetty, devouring an ice-cream, and driving past grain silos on the road from Adelaide, all the time nagging 'how long 'til we get there?' All of these elements help to make it a wonderful place to get away from it all.

Tips From the Crew

- Lisa says if you're after a breathtaking view, drive a couple of kilometres into Innes National Park. You'll be swept away by the rugged coastline and views out to Kangaroo Island.

- Jeff recommends taking your boogie board and fins to experience the beautiful 'bottom-end' beaches,

but warns to watch out for rips and undertows.

- Ron loves the large collection of photographs and artefacts relating to the windjammer era in the Port Victoria National Trust Museum. Divers interested in exploring the eight shipwrecks off this part of the coast can buy a waterproof map of the Wardang Island Maritime Heritage Trail from The Environment Shop in Adelaide

- Trevor our sound man claims his most asked question is: 'What's that big fluffy thing?' He explains that it's a windsock designed to reduce noise to the microphone. The fluff on the outside helps to dissipate the wind. Trev's tip for home-video buffs is to buy a child's foam indoor ball, cut in some cross slots and insert the mike. It's a cheap and effective way of reducing wind noise on protruding microphones – and it can get pretty windy on Yorkes!

Keith at Stenhouse Bay   Photo by Andrew McEvoy

The numerous jetties that punctuate Yorke Peninsula's coastline are reminders of the tall sailing ships and smaller ketches that once called in to collect cereal and wool. You'll see visible signs of shipwrecks along the coast, and much more beneath the waves on an amazing Maritime Heritage Trail that takes in sunken wrecks and breathtaking scenery.

Copper was discovered on the peninsula in the late 1850s and the towns of Kadina, Moonta and Wallaroo became known as the Copper Triangle. Their mines brought thousands of people into the area from all over the world. Visitors can tour what's left of the mines and grab a Cornish pasty, a delicious legacy of the families who came to South Australia from Cornwall in the mining heyday. The world's largest Cornish festival, Kernewek Lowender, enlivens Yorke Peninsula every two years with traditional singing and dancing, literary events and a cavalcade of cars and motorcycles.

... if you drive right down to the bottom, you'll be rewarded with a little piece of paradise.

You can fish and swim in great spots all along the coast, and if you drive right down to the bottom of the peninsula's 'foot', you'll be rewarded with a piece of paradise. Innes National Park is a rugged, scrubby idyll with isolated beaches, towering cliffs,

I Didn't Know That!

- Caroline Carleton, who wrote the words to the 'Song of Australia', was buried in the local cemetery at Wallaroo on 12 July 1874. You'll find an obelisk erected in her honour in the town's Centenary Square.

- Just off Edithburgh you can stay on your very own island – Troubridge Island. There's a light-keeper's cottage, sandy beaches and fairy penguins.

- Possum Kipling, of Redex Trial driving fame, started the first roadhouse (affectionately known as 'Possum's') in Port Wakefield in the 1950s.

- The rangers at Innes National Park run seasonal activities for adults and kids including rock-pool rambles, Aboriginal culture explorations, and historic walks around Inneston Village.

- You can catch a fisherman's basket on the Yorke Peninsula: snapper, garfish, salmon, squid, King George whiting, tommy ruff, mullet, flathead, and blue swimmer crabs. Yum!

The Dee brothers grow Pacific oysters in the gulf off Stansbury

Shipwreck at Innes National Park
Photo by Andrew McEvoy

spectacular views, great fishing and camping, and legendary surf beaches. If you're after more history, the ghost town of Inneston, within the park, is a great place to wander among the ruins and learn about another mining town.

Yorke Peninsula is a reasonably quick drive from Adelaide. You can hop in the car on a Friday night, stop for coffee and petrol at Port Wakefield on your way through, and get to most destinations within two or three hours. As you drive through Port Wakefield's rows of petrol stations and food stops, bear in mind that it once was a real port. A tidal inlet was discovered in the mangroves in the 1800s and an instant port was established to ship the copper ore brought down by bullock from Burra. Why not pull off the main road and explore the old part of historic Port Wakefield?

Crabbing, mining, lighthouses, bird-watching, surfing, boating, walking and eating oysters – we enjoyed Yorke Peninsula, and you will too.

Want More Information?

SA Visitor and Travel Centre
1300 366 770

Yorke Peninsula Visitor Centre – Moonta
1800 654 991

Yorke Peninsula Visitor Centre – Minlaton
(08) 8853 2600

Yorke Peninsula website
www.yorkepeninsula.com.au

The Environment Shop
(08) 8204 1910

National Parks and Wildlife SA
(08) 8854 3200

RAA Touring (maps and guides)
(08) 8205 4540

SA Tourism Commission website
www.southaustralia.com.au

Postcards website
www.postcards.sa.com.au

Althorpe Island

with Ron Kandelaars

The sun was just rising at Marion Bay as we climbed aboard a charter boat for a pilgrimage to Althorpe Island, which sits between the tip of Yorke Peninsula and Kangaroo Island. The reefs and islands around this part of the peninsula have claimed many lives and there are constant reminders of how dangerous these waters can be. We saw the rudder post of a wreck, the *Wilyama*, as we made our way past Rhino Head and, nearby, the spot where the *Pareora* went down, along with her captain and ten crew.

Althorpe Island sits between the tip of Yorke Peninsula and Kangaroo Island   Photo by Bernd Stoecker

As we passed Althorpe Island's seal colony and headed towards the jetty, John Lawley, a former lighthouse-keeper, and son of a lighthouse-keeper, reminisced about coming to the island as a nine-year-old:

'It was a place of adventure. I remember that as a young child. I always get that same feeling coming back.'

Michael Lucieer joined us for the pilgrimage. He was one of the last keepers to work on the island in 1991, and now he and John are members of the Friends of Althorpe Island Conservation Park.

As the boat pulled in to the island, the prospect of hauling supplies up a ninety-metre cliff brought home the remoteness of this place. It's a climb that keepers have made ever since the lighthouse was built in 1879. Althorpe was first discovered by the French explorer Nicholas Baudin, who named it Isles Vauban. Matthew Flinders also came across this amazing layer of limestone in 1802 and called it Omicron Island. Twelve years later it was re-named Althorpe after the Viscount of Althorpe in England, a distant ancestor of the late Princess Diana. Late last century fear of invasion by the Russians prompted the laying of a telegraph cable to Althorpe Island so that the keepers could scan the waters and maintain contact with the mainland.

The lighthouse is now fully automated but in the old days three keepers lived here with their families. When you look down the steep cliff from the cottages to the beach, you get a sense of what it must have felt like for them. Although John Lawley remembers his childhood adventures fondly, he says it's one adventure to stay here on holiday and quite another to live and work here.

'It's hard to imagine a more isolated place. If things went wrong with the flying fox to the jetty below, your only lifeline was effectively gone.'

In the late 1800s sixty men were employed to hang on slings to dig a cutting in the cliff face. Some of the workers were accused of not pulling their weight, and an industrial dispute ensued. Conditions were poor, and one night, while the men slept on the beach, a foreman was killed when a rock 'accidentally' fell on his tent.

Althorpe Island can still be dangerous today. Visitors need to keep to the paths and be careful where they wander. John still remembers the day when, as a nine-year-old, he stumbled across the entrance to a blow-hole at the top of an ocean cave. He lowered himself by rope into the chamber below and fell into the swirling sea. Fortunately, he swam among the seals to safety.

Althorpe Island lighthouse, built in 1879

Photo by Keith Conlon

Wherever you wander on Althorpe Island, you'll find stunning views. To the south, rugged cliffs on the north coast of Kangaroo Island. Further west, a distant lighthouse at Cape Borda and, further still, magnificent Wedge Island. To the north, Innes National Park from West Cape all the way to Cape Spencer and beyond.

We left John and Michael to enjoy the island and caught the charter boat back to the mainland. You can get to Althorpe Island with Davenport Fishing Charters. To stay overnight here, join the Friends of Althorpe Island Conservation Park.

Friends of Althorpe Island
Conservation Park
Contact John Lawley
Tel (08) 8528 5265

Davenport Fishing Charters
Contact Andrew Donslarr
Tel 0417 854 578

Althorpe
Island

Southern Yorke Oysters
with Ron Kandelaars

For brothers Paul, Michael and Damian Dee commuting to work takes on a different meaning. Each morning they set off from the jetty at Stansbury on Yorke Peninsula for another day at the office. Out in Gulf St Vincent, you can spot Mount Lofty well into the distance and the water tower at Stansbury seems a long way off. There's a beacon about four kilometres off the coast, and Paul says that the water is so shallow in summer, you can almost walk all the way out to it.

The Pacific oyster takes three years to mature

The three brothers' work is the culmination of a dream. They grow Pacific oysters out in the gulf, and today we've come to check on their progress. Unfortunately for the Dee boys, the coldest days of winter are their busiest times. In fact, the colder the better, because cold air interacts with the shell and creates a fattening process. So it's not uncommon for them to be working in icy temperatures of two degrees or so.

Aquaculture is one of this state's rising industries and it has surprising similarities to another South Australian boom enterprise. The Dees string up baskets on black line using posts and clips, very much as you'd find in a vineyard. They click the line down so the oysters can grow gently below the wave action. When it's time to fatten the oysters, they're lifted to the next clip so that they sit at a good height in the food chain and get a gentle rumble from the wave action.

This chilly work has obvious compensations. Yet while the Pacific oyster may be an instant taste sensation, there's nothing instant about its development from tiny spat to luscious plump edible. Maturation takes around three years, but the potential outcome is hundreds of thousands of oysters.

Southern Yorke Oysters now export their treasures to Hong Kong. Keep your eye out for the Dee boys sorting through the latest batch of oysters any afternoon after 1 pm.

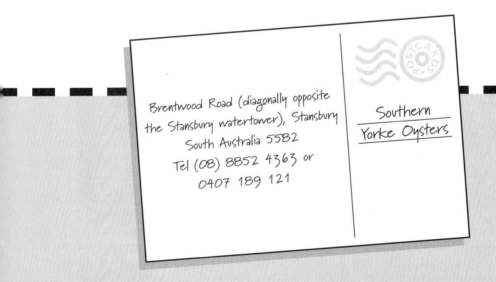

Brentwood Road (diagonally opposite the Stansbury watertower), Stansbury South Australia 5582
Tel (08) 8852 4363 or 0407 189 121

Southern Yorke Oysters

Moonta Heritage Trails
with Keith Conlon

Once, enormous mines operated day and night, proclaiming South Australia as the copper kingdom of the world. Now there is only the sound of the wind and birds as you look out over the Moonta Mines.

A copper mine was established at nearby Wallaroo more than one-hundred-and-forty years ago, and was quickly followed by the Moonta Mining Company. Today, it is difficult to fathom the size of it all. Seventeen-hundred men and boys worked at the mine in around-the-clock shifts. A handsome town quickly grew, and the population swelled to ten-thousand souls – many of them Cornish families who'd come to the town from the Burra mine in South Australia's Mid North or from the depressed south-west of England.

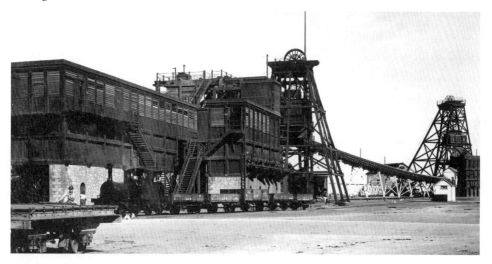

South Australia was once the copper kingdom of the world

Our *Postcards* tour began at the gracious Moonta Town Hall, the departure point for two excellent heritage trails. Walking along, munching on fabulous Cornish pasties, we noticed that the miners' Methodist faith didn't stop Moonta from having its fair share of

Seventeen-hundred men and boys worked at the Moonta mine in around-the-clock shifts

pubs. On the town trail you pass an antique shop that was once the Prince of Wales Hotel. Cock-fights were held out the back in the early days. Down the block, the Moonta Hotel is still operating. Both buildings have been here since the town began in 1863, and dozens of classic stone buildings went up during the rich 1860s and 1870s.

We climbed aboard the Moonta Tourist Train, which snakes its way past the ruins of copper-processing plants and through a tunnel under tailings dumps, or 'Moonta's Himalayas', as they used to be called.

As the train passes Ryan's Shaft, give a thought to shepherd Patrick Ryan, who first found a chunk of copper ore in a wombat hole here. What the memorial stone for Paddy Ryan doesn't mention is that he told not only his boss, landowner Walter Watson Hughes, but also the Port Wakefield publican. A race to register the mining leases followed and it took years to resolve the dispute between the parties. Now there are only glimpses of the great mining operation left at the site.

In parts, the native scrub has returned to soften the mine area mess. It must have looked like a lunar landscape with a mine on top. I climbed another tailings dump, this one named after legendary mine manager Captain Hancock. Giant flat-topped piles of dusty red sand are all that's left of the one-and-a-half million tonnes raised from the tunnel labyrinth beneath. Below Hancock's Heap is the Woods family cottage, a survivor of the hundreds of cottages that grew higgledy-piggledy between the shaftheads. It is now nurtured by the National Trust.

A quaintly rustic church sits at the end of a side road further along the Mine Trail. The Moonta Mines Methodist Church was built in 1865 to replace a hut version. The mighty Hughes Engine-house, several stories high in local stone, and accompanied by its tall round chimney, has also been saved. The tower housed a huge Cornish steam engine that pumped water to keep the mines dry.

The Elder lode ran north nearly one kilometre from here. It was named after Sir Thomas Elder, who no doubt used some of his incredible dividends to fund his donations to the Art Gallery, the Adelaide University Music School and the Elder Park Rotunda. Add to this the donation by mine principal Walter Watson Hughes that was so substantial it gave rise to the city's first university and you can say, fairly, that there's more than a little bit of Moonta in Adelaide.

The boys who worked the mine did not share in the wealth. They were paid a shilling a week. Many of them, however, went to the new Moonta Mines School when it opened in 1878. Grand and gothic in style, one thousand students were enrolled there in the town's heyday. Today it's a National Trust Museum.

You can also visit the Wheat Hughes Mine, just north of the town, and catch a compelling glimpse of mining old and new. Moonta has an excellent Visitors' Information Centre in the old railway station, and its heritage trails booklet is packed with information that brings the rich history of the town alive.

Moonta Visitors' Information Centre
Old Railway Station, Moonta
South Australia 5558
Tel (08) 8825 1891
Open every day 9 am–5 pm

Moonta
Heritage Trails

Innes National Park

with Keith Conlon

Innes National Park is a rugged coastal wilderness at the 'tippy-toe' end of the Yorke Peninsula foot. It was dedicated as a national park in 1972 to protect the rare great western whipbird and named after William Innes, who discovered gypsum here in the 1890s.

As we stood next to the modern navigational light high on the cliffs at Cape Spencer, with Althorpe Island gleaming in the winter sun in Investigator Strait, a sense of timelessness overtook us.

Young English navigator Matthew Flinders first plotted the charts for this spectacular coast. He named Yorke Peninsula after a former colleague at sea, and the Cape after Lord Spencer in the Admiralty.

We spotted several groups of emus during our visit to Innes National Park   Photo by Trevor Griscti

Innes National Park attracts 150,000 people or more a year. Some come to sense the drama and danger of the seventy-metre cliffs and ancient seabeds. Bird-watchers search for the elusive great western whipbird, while heritage hunters head for the old mining town of Inneston and its port at Stenhouse Bay. Surfing, fishing and camping lure others to the park.

Across a beautiful cove, West Cape rises defiantly towards the Southern Ocean, with two-billion-year-old base rocks projecting into the surf. Take a short walk around the headland and you'll discover magnificent Pondalowie Bay sheltered behind two large islands. Throughout summer you'll find cray-boats moored there overnight, not far from an idyllic shack town in the sand-dunes. Further round, 'Pondy' is regarded as one of the best wave breaks within easy reach of Adelaide.

The local clan of the Narangga people called the place Pandalawi, meaning rocky waterhole. It was good fishing for them too, and they supplemented their diet with kangaroos they'd herd onto small peninsulas to club and spear. We spotted several groups of kangaroos and emus during our visit.

The pristine and thick mallee scrub of Innes National Park is broken by large salt lakes. They've been mined for gypsum and salt for more than a century and remnants of the mining ghost town of Inneston remain today. Gypsum was transported from

Inneston to the port of Stenhouse Bay by horse-drawn railway. The port was killed off when the first good road was extended to the tip of Yorke Peninsula in 1960 and now forms part of Innes National Park.

The last ships called in 1972, but evidence of the Peninsula's seafaring history remains. The *Hougomont* was scuttled just off the cape at Stenhouse Bay in 1932. Its service as a breakwater is long gone, but it's now part of a maritime heritage diving trail along this coast. The Norwegian barque *Ethel*, an icon of Innes National Park, was washed onto a narrow cliff beach here in a January storm in 1904. Once an intact ship, it's now crumpled on the sand. In 1920 the coastal steamer *Ferret* ground ashore in a fog. The ship's boiler pokes out of the sand in winter, adding more fascination to the 'bottom end' of the Yorke Peninsula.

Chinaman's Hat is a popular surfing spot within the park. A specially constructed boardwalk protects the fragile coastal environment here and allows visitors to walk safely down the cliff face. We could have stayed for hours on the cliff-top 'balcony' watching the surfers play Russian roulette with the pounding surf and a limestone reef. But we left them to their sport and headed inland along the boardwalk.

Innes National Park is a spectacular destination. For a sense of solitude, try getting there off-season. There are well-planned camping grounds or you can hire one of a range of cottages and houses from National Parks and Wildlife SA. The Park head-quarters is at Stenhouse Bay and you can get petrol, supplies and food at the general store and tavern there.

Stenhouse Bay
South Australia 5577
Tel (08) 8854 3200

Innes
National Park

Ardrossan Crabs

with Lisa McAskill

rdrossan has two dominant features: one is a grain bulk-handling facility with the largest elevator tower in the state at seventy metres high; the other is the twenty-five-metre clay cliffs that separate the town from Gulf St Vincent.

Ardrossan sits on the east coast of the peninsula, about ninety minutes from Adelaide and most workers in the town are involved in shipping grain or dolomite. But our mission in Ardrossan was to get among the blue swimmer crabs that love the shallows beneath the red cliffs. A good rule of thumb is to remember that crabs are best in months that have the letter 'r' in them, so March and April are terrific, but don't get any ideas about out-crabbing anyone from Ardrossan. We enlisted the help of Mark Hicks who runs the Royal House Hotel Motel. Mark's been crabbing so long that locals say he gets out of bed sideways.

Pulling a crab rake through the water is not as easy as it looks. As we scraped the sand in search of *Portunus pelagicus*, we felt like chooks scratching round for a feed. Marks says the action wakes the crabs and they react by clawing onto the rake. Next, it's a matter of flipping the crabs into a floating fishing bucket. If they get stuck, Mark offers some sage advice:

'Just grab 'em. But you better watch out, sometimes they fight back!'

Mark Hicks has been crabbing so long that the locals say he gets out of bed sideways

Blue swimmer crabs love the shallows beneath Ardrossan's red cliffs

Even though the waters here seem littered with 'blues', there are rules to crabbing and everyone needs a measurer. The small ones must be thrown back, which means they'll be there waiting for you next year.

We were close to our bag limit of forty crabs per person when we ambled back to Mark's pub where our catch was put into boiling water. Eating crabs isn't the most civilised dining but it may be close to the most agreeable – especially fresh from the gulf.

In addition to offering crab cooking and eating facilities, the Royal House has motel units, cabins and pub rooms at reasonable prices. Free with the room comes the best information on crab hot spots.

Contact Mark Hicks
Tel (08) 8837 3007

Royal House
Hotel Motel,
Ardrossan

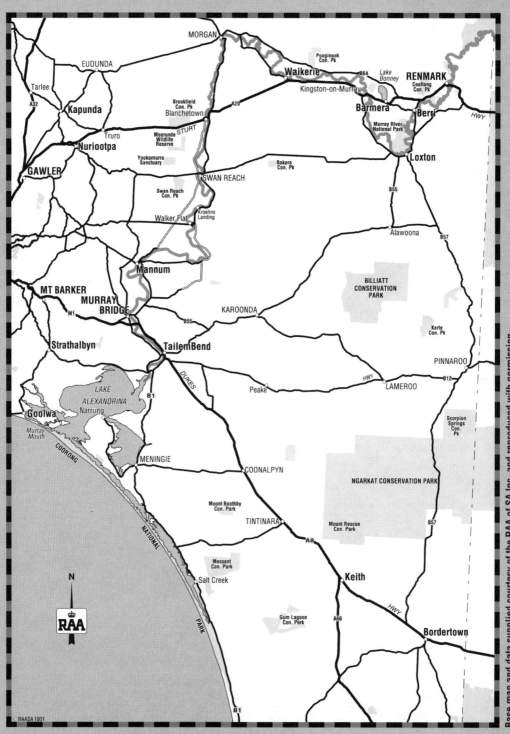

Reverse: River Murray Big Bend Photo by Pete Dobre

They say that once you've drunk the water, you're hooked.

Dusk fishing on the Murray   Photo by Mick Bradley

The Border Cliffs, three-hundred-and-sixty-five kilometres upstream from the Murray Mouth, let the river-boat captains know they were heading into South Australia. The Murray River has changed dramatically since those rollicking days. But somehow the great muddy waterway has echoed those times ever since.

Just past the Border Cliffs, twenty kilometres by road from the citrus fruit and grape growing town of Renmark, is the old Customs House, a classic piece of pre-Federation history. Originally it was an office of the colonial bureaucracy where agents collected duty from the passing paddle-steamers. Today it's a friendly supply-post where you can hire a canoe and head off into a looping system of wetland creeks. As you paddle, watch out for the grotesque fallen giants and centuries-old river red gums.

Tips From the Crew

- Lisa enjoys soaring through the sky at the Waikerie Gliding Club and then dropping into Country Cuisine at Ramco for dried apricots dipped in chocolate.

- Jeff says the Nildottie Cliffs at sunset are stunning. He also recommends hiring a canoe and exploring the backwaters.

- Keith recommends dressing warm (scarf, hat and gloves) if you're heading to Banrock Station for an early morning walk.

- Ron says you'd be a mug not to take a fishing rod with you. He says you can do the river a favour by catching pesky carp and feeding it to the pelicans. He also suggests a camel ride with the Bush Safari Co. along the river to the 'Dromedary Point' Cliff-top Restaurant.

- Trevor says the best oranges and mandarines he's ever tasted were from the Moorook Cottages. (He says it makes a change from snacking on Barbecue Shapes when he's driving with Jeff!) He also recommends a ride on the ex-rocket launcher at Portee Station as long as you don't take the dog's seat!

Pelicans at Banrock Station

The River Murray, with its houseboating, fishing, water-skiing, walking trails and wildlife can be an adventure holiday or a tranquil retreat, depending on how you like it. Many boaties take the epic journey from historic Wellington at one end to Murray Bridge, Mannum, the cliffs of Nildottie, the former inland port of Morgan, along the Riverland towns of Waikerie, Loxton, Berri and Renmark and then up to the border. It's a fantastic, invigorating trip.

Along the way you'll experience the diversity of a river steeped in history and abundant in wildlife. Thick, untamed mallee meets wetlands brimming with bird-life on the Murray. Majestic limestone cliffs and river red gums line the mighty waterway providing spectacular scenery at any time of the day, from the eerie misty mornings to the blazing evening sunsets.

Environmental issues are top of the agenda these days along the Murray. Across the country you'll hear talk of the Bookmark Biosphere environment project and regeneration of wetlands at Banrock and Akuna stations, as well as the problematic issue of salinity. Landowners, governments and passionate locals alike are making a big effort to ensure that the mighty Murray's natural environment lives on. But there's always more to be done. As you enjoy this imposing waterway, make sure you're part of the solution, not the problem. Don't throw anything into our fragile Murray.

I Didn't Know That!

- Captain Charles Sturt and his whaleboat crew, in 1830, were the first white men to journey down the River Murray.

- There are nine sunken paddlesteamers and barges in the river at Murray Bridge.

- There are eleven species of frog found in the lower River Murray, including the Mallee spadefoot and the barking marsh frog.

- Mid February through to winter is generally the best time for fishing in the Murray.

- Two brothers from Canada, George and William Chaffey, established Australia's first irrigation settlement in Renmark, the oldest town in the region.

- At the Cobdogla Irrigation and Steam Museum, the gas-driven Humphrey Pump is the only working model left in the world.

The Riverland region stretches from Blanchetown to Paringa. Over ninety per cent of the state's citrus, stone fruit and nuts are produced here. Proving that South Australia really is the wine state, Berri Estates at Glossop is Australia's largest winery and distillery, and many smaller wine producers have now made their mark on the industry, putting the Riverland well and truly on the world's wine map.

At Barmera, shallow Lake Bonney is popular for aquatic sports. Barmera comes alive every June as it hosts the SA Country Music Festival. At nearby Berri, you can follow the riverfront on a two-kilometre walking trail that stretches from the town's bridge to Martin's Bend, a favourite spot for picnics, fishing and skiing. Further north, Monash Adventure Park has flying foxes, a rope bridge, a giant maze and landscaped waterfalls and streams.

If you want history, you'll find it everywhere. Long before white settlement, Aboriginal culture blossomed for thousands of years in this region. At the Ngaut Ngaut Conservation Park near Swan Reach, archaeologists have found Aboriginal engravings

that pre-date the Nile pharoahs and pyramids. To learn about the Murray's bygone river-trading days, visit the port of Morgan with its restored wharf, and a riverboat museum. Just out of Morgan you'll find a fascinating fossil quarry, and a little further on at the Nor'West Bend Museum, there's a blacksmith shop and old general store.

So sit back, throw a line and enjoy our *Postcards* from the River Murray.

Lisa hitches a ride on a the *Mayflower* near Morgan   Photo by Jeff Clayfield

Need More Information?

SA Visitor and Travel Centre
1300 655 276

Riverland Hotline
1300 657 625

Riverland website
www.riverland.net.au

Mallee Tourist and Heritage Centre
(08) 8577 8644

National Parks and Wildlife SA
(08) 8576 3690

RAA Touring (maps and guides)
(08) 8205 4540

SA Tourism Commission website
www.southaustralia.com

Postcards **website**
www.postcards.sa.com

Fishing on the Murray
with Ron Kandelaars

The River Murray is the oldest commercial fishery in South Australia and for third-generation commercial fisher Shane Warwick the recent haul has been extremely good. The view from his tinnie on the river at Walker Flat seems hard to beat, particularly on a warm afternoon, but he says it's not so much fun in the middle of winter.

Each early morning and late afternoon, Shane heads out along the river to check a series of drum nets, probably the most popular net used in commercial river fishery. Today, like a rabbit out of a hat, he plucks a twenty-pound Murray cod from a net. With cod, there's a minimum size limit of fifty centimetres and a maximum size limit too – just over a metre. The biggies over that are the mega-spawners, as Shane likes to call them, and they're crucial to the ongoing survival of the river's cod population.

There's nothing bigger than a Murray cod in this river; they're the major predator, perched at the top of the food chain. If you're wondering why you've never caught one while dangling a line, then consider this: scientific trials have indicated that cod can go for up to five years without feeding. During long dry spells, and before the advent of locks and weirs, the river was at times just a series of unconnected ponds. A super-efficient predator like the Murray cod would have cleaned out his pond and waited, sometimes several years, before floods brought more water and food.

At thirty dollars a kilogram a beast like this fetches good money. Shane says that now there's a four-month closed season on Murray cod, it's not unusual for commercial fishers to put back three to four hundred of them during that time. But he's not complaining. He says it gives you a good feeling to let them go, knowing there'll be more Murray cod for the future.

Wherever Shane goes, the pelicans follow. These feathery hangers-on fly in for a feed off one of the river's major pests – European carp – or anything else they can scavenge. Shane knows them well:

'This is "Tiny", a little bloke who's put on some conditioning thanks to the fishers. The one behind is "Guts" and I think you know why. He's the gamest and the one who comes in closest.'

Shane Warwick and Keith haul in a prized Murray cod

'Guts' was circling as we left Shane to check his other nets. By late in the day it was obvious why this river life runs deep in the Warwick clan. Three generations have now sampled the mystical Murray existence.

For fishing size and bag limits, along with further information, call the Department of Primary Industries and Resources or visit their website. Riverland fishing shops, including Hook, Line and Sinker in Denny Street, Berri, can also help with fishing information and tackle.

Contact Department of Primary
Industries and Resources
Tel (08) 8226 2311
website www.pir.sa.gov.au/fishing

Fishing
on the
Murray

Kroehn's Landing Boardwalk

with Ron Kandelaars

As houseboats edge along the cliffs downstream from Swan Reach, they pass one of the most important archaeological sites in Australia, or anywhere. Under a shade cloth at the end of a boardwalk you come to a limestone overhang, and it seems like a logical place for the river's earliest human inhabitants to have met, escaped the rain and cooked a feed.

Nganguraku guide Richard Hunter says this place is the history book of the Indigenous people of Australia. Each layer of charcoal, animal bone and shell grit is another chapter in an epic story. The overhanging cliffs at what is now called Ngaut Ngaut Conservation Park were once a great meeting place for clans from all over the place. It was here that they'd talk and settle disputes. River people traded their goods for ceremonial ochre or granite pieces for tools.

Back in the late 1920s, South Australian Museum archaeologists discovered a seven-thousand-year-old skeleton of a young boy at the Devon Downs archaeological site here. From then on our understanding of the place changed forever. Richard says:

'They came out here in 1929 and 1930, and what they found really excited them, literally excited the world. It put Australia on the world map of archaeology.'

It's the most significant archaeological site in South Australia thanks to anthropologist Norman Tindale and his offsider Hale, who sank their trenches down through centuries of river history. In one location the pair dug down approximately six metres through many layers of the remains of fires. As they delved deeper, they reached engravings that have now been carbon dated to eight thousand years ago.

It's a staggering thought. Engravings that predate the pharoahs and pyramids on the Nile, left by people who camped here on the banks of the Murray thousands of years ago. For anyone interested in the ancient history of our land, a visit to Kroehn's Landing is a must. You can join a boardwalk tour run by local Nganguraku people. Call the National Parks and Wildlife Service for details.

Opposite: Kroehn's Landing, one of Australia's most important archaeological sites
Right: Nganguraku guide Richard Hunter

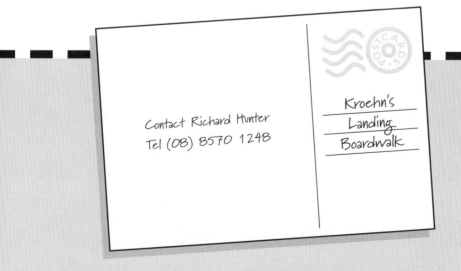

Contact Richard Hunter
Tel (08) 8570 1248

Kroehn's
Landing
Boardwalk

Banrock Station Boardwalk Trail
with Lisa McAskill

anrock Station is a venture into a unique blend of winemaking and environmental regeneration.

From the patio of its Wine and Wetland Centre you can absorb a tranquil vista of the mallee and River Murray floodplains below. A new Boardwalk Trail allows visitors to get closer to the wetlands and wildlife on the floodplain. Out there, it's a haven for bird-life, but there's plenty of work to be done. Wetlands are among the most vital, productive and diverse ecosystems on the planet, and nowhere are they more important than in a dry continent like Australia.

As the locks and weirs turned the Murray into a series of huge ponds, the original wetlands either drowned under too much water or died of thirst – and now regular floods don't come either. Yet from the tasting room the Banrock Station wetlands look

Banrock Station is a unique blend of winemaking and environmental regeneration

a picture of health. At the downstream end a 'wetland doctor' has recreated a vital part of the cure – sluice gates. Tony Sharley, the manager of Banrock Station, says the gates not only allow staff to raise the level of the water in the wetland and create a much-needed flood, but they also allow the system to dry out, which is crucial when restoring a wetland. Tony explains:

'All we're doing is simulating the natural process that all of our wildlife has adapted to. The stimulus to breeding for most of our plants and animals is actually to have a dry wetlands system followed by floods – all of a sudden you've got this great cue for breeding. There's lots of life around, lots of nutrients, a smorgasbord of food, and conditions are right for growth.'

As the bulrushes return, so does the marine life, along with hundreds of bird species. The wetting and drying of wetlands replicates what once took place here for thousands of years.

Tony and his team are returning what's been taken away since European settlement – another pet project is the planting of twenty kilometres of trenches with direct seeding gathered from five kilometres around. Judging by the growth of seeds planted a year ago, it's safe to say the mallee is on its way back at Banrock Station.

It's best to book in advance for the Banrock Station Boardwalk Trail. There are four walks a day, beginning at 7 am. You'll be hungry when you return and the restaurant at The Wine and Wetland Centre offers an alfresco-style menu using native Australian ingredients.

Holmes Road, Kingston-On-Murray
South Australia 5331
Tel (08) 85 830 299
website www.banrockstation.com.au
Open every day, bookings essential,
7 kilometre trail
(approximately 3 hours' walk)

Banrock
Station
Boardwalk
Trail

Bush and Backwaters Tours
with Ron Kandelaars

Above: We climbed aboard a flat-bottomed 'tinnie' and twisted our way up Ral Ral Creek   Photo by Jeff Clayfield

Opposite: Afternoon light streams through the redgums

It's not hard to sell the virtues of a houseboat cruise on the River Murray. But if you're heading upstream from Renmark, you must also take a trip into the creeks and less-travelled backwaters. *Postcards* hitched a ride with Joe Cresp, a former engineering workshop owner who yearned to be close to nature. Joe has been running his Bush and Backwaters Tours with his wife, Tricia, for five years.

Joe quickly slid a flat-bottomed 'tinnie' into Ral Ral Creek and, with the late afternoon light streaming through red gums lined up like pickets on the banks, we twisted our way up the creek and into a secret world. Close by we spotted an Aboriginal canoe tree, and around the bend a burnt-out tree trunk. Joe explained that most burnt-out trees are the result of lightning strikes, but are occasionally caused by campers or houseboat ramblers who build fires too close to the bush.

Joe's visitors are taken into mysterious backwaters, with names to match: the Ral Ral, the Amazon, and the Big and Little Hunchee, amongst others. Technically, they are 'anabranches', smaller streams that depart the main course of the Murray to return many kilometres downstream.

Joe argues passionately that more water needs to be allocated to these areas from the upstream storages of the Murray–Darling system.

'The value of the water to these floodplains is that it creates a life-cycle of the plant and animal life. Without it, the system will die.'

The Bookmark Biosphere Trust, an internationally recognised environmental organisation committed to conserving natural habitats through research, has endorsed Joe, along with a handful of other educated and responsible operators, to take tour groups into this delicate conservation park wilderness.

We drifted on a vast shallow lagoon watching flights of wood duck and marvelling at the sunset through a line of red gums on a distant bank. Nearby, a wallaby watched us glide by from his perch on a green boggy clearing. Joe says many of his English guests find the surrounds quite desolate, just as Captain Charles Sturt did in 1830. But most tourists, including the many Australians who hitch a ride on Joe's boat, are in awe of this watery wonderland. And, as we found, it doesn't come any more moving, or peaceful, than drifting on the backwaters at dusk.

Contact Joe and Tricia Cresp
Tel/Fax (08) 8586 5344
email bbwaters@riverland.net.au

Bush and
Backwaters
Tours

Mannum's River History
with Keith Conlon

Today's luxurious rivercraft allow their passengers to cruise the Murray in style – a far cry from the spartan conditions of Captain Charles Sturt's 1830 whale-boat expedition. As he explored the river Sturt rowed downstream until he found the green slopes of what is now Mannum. It impressed him so much that he wrote about it in his journals, inspiring the dreams of London bankers and philosophers who were looking for a new colony.

During the flood of 1956 one side of Mannum's main street was under water

I can't look at the main street of Mannum without thinking of the great flood of 1956. One side of the main street was underwater completely. It was a canal for months on end and thousands of people drove up here to marvel at the power of the river, and lend a hand to locals whose houses and businesses were beset by a watery seige.

A scenic lookout provides a view over the town that legendary Captain William Randell, a Gumeracha flour miller, helped to prosperity. A canny fellow, he wanted to sell bags of flour to the hungry hordes at the new Victorian goldfields – so, just upstream from here, in 1853, he built the Murray's first ever paddlesteamer, the *Mary Ann*. You can still see its boiler in the local Mannum Museum. His former home, Randell House, overlooks the river that he turned into the Mississippi-down-under.

The PS *Marion* is moored at Mannum to remind us of those days. For one-hundred-and-three years now, she's paddled up and down the river. You can still get aboard this fully restored paddlesteamer and cruise past willows and pelicans.

Prime Minister Andrew Fisher was on board in 1915, and he described it as a beautiful and exhilarating trip. Another member of parliament around this time called our river 'the Nile of Australia' and he further declared that:

'The Australian who has not been afloat on the waters of the Murray does not know his country.'

He said it, and I hope you can get afloat sometime soon on the marvellous Murray.

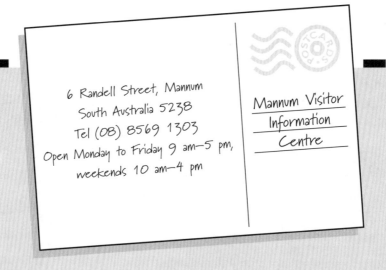

6 Randell Street, Mannum
South Australia 5238
Tel (08) 8569 1303
Open Monday to Friday 9 am—5 pm,
weekends 10 am—4 pm

Mannum Visitor
Information
Centre

Limestone Coast

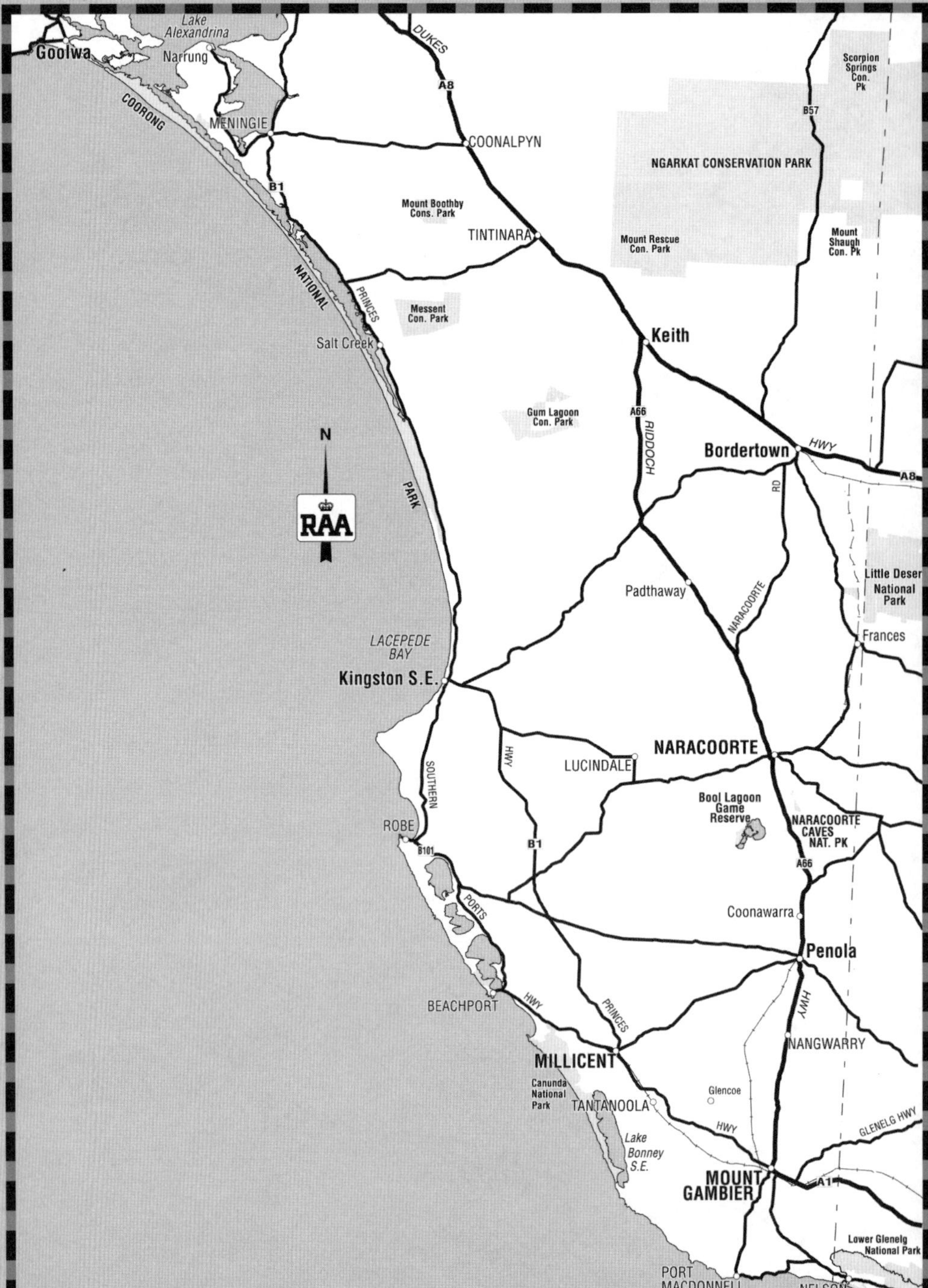

Goolwa
Lake Alexandrina
Narrung
COORONG
MENINGIE
NATIONAL
PRINCES
B1
DUKES
A8
COONALPYN
Mount Boothby Cons. Park
TINTINARA
Messent Con. Park
Salt Creek
Gum Lagoon Con. Park
Keith
A66
RIDDOCH
Mount Rescue Con. Park
NGARKAT CONSERVATION PARK
Scorpion Springs Con. Pk
B57
Mount Shaugh Con. Pk
Bordertown
HWY
A8
RD
Little Desert National Park
N
RAA
PARK
Padthaway
NARACOORTE
Frances
LACEPEDE BAY
Kingston S.E.
SOUTHERN
HWY
LUCINDALE
NARACOORTE
Bool Lagoon Game Reserve
NARACOORTE CAVES NAT. PK
A66
ROBE
B101
B1
PORTS
Coonawarra
Penola
BEACHPORT
HWY
PRINCES
HWY
NANGWARRY
MILLICENT
Canunda National Park
TANTANOOLA
Glencoe
Lake Bonney S.E.
HWY
GLENELG HWY
MOUNT GAMBIER
A1
PORT MACDONNELL
NELSON
Lower Glenelg National Park
© RAASA1001

Base map and data supplied courtesy of the RAA of SA Inc. and reproduced with permission

Reverse: Guichen Bay, Robe   Photo by Pete Dobre

A region that was once the floor of the Southern Ocean.

ount Gambier's Blue Lake, the Naracoorte Caves World Heritage Area, the crumbly red dirt of the Coonawarra region, and the delicately balanced ecosystem of the Coorong – these are South Australian icons, unique to a region that was once the floor of the Southern Ocean.

Mount Gambier's Blue Lake   Photo by Andrew McEvoy

The Limestone Coast was formed from sediment that built up on the seabed over millions of years. Eventually the ocean retired to further afield, leaving a limestone bedrock behind. This geological history explains many of the Limestone Coast's features today: labyrinth-like cave systems, terra rossa soil, sinkholes, aquifers, and significant fossil discoveries that have changed the way we view our world.

Tips From the Crew

- Lisa suggests you take a ride on the Limestone Coast railway. It departs Mount Gambier and travels through pine forests and farm country to the Coonawarra region and Penola, one of the region's oldest settlements.

- Keith recommends a night visit to the beautifully terraced and floodlit gardens of Mount Gambier's Umpherston Sinkhole where you can feed the possums. And while you're in Mount Gambier don't miss the Aquifer Blue Lake Tour.

- Ron says next time you're visiting the Limestone Coast, look upwards at night. The wide open spaces make for wonderful starry nights.

- Trevor always takes an early morning walk on Robe's Long Beach.

Some of the oldest Aboriginal engravings and finger markings in the world have been found in caves near Mount Gambier.

Diving at Piccaninnie Ponds

Some of the oldest Aboriginal engravings and finger markings in the world have been found in caves near Mount Gambier, confirming that indigenous people have lived in the area for eons. The Ngarrindjeri people have lived in the Coorong for over six thousand years and called the area Karangh, meaning long narrow neck. Today, these people have a strong involvement in the cultural heritage of the area. The 145 kilometre long Coorong National Park is a beautiful stretch with an amazing array of wildlife, including hundreds of species of birds.

The Limestone Coast is perfect for fishing, swimming, boating, snorkelling and diving. You can explore a choice of National Parks that include wetlands, bushlands, coastline and caves. And no

I Didn't Know That!

- There are agreements in place with the governments of China and Japan to help protect the Coorong's migratory birds.

- Penola was once home to poets Adam Lindsay Gordon, John Shaw Neilson and Will Ogilvie. Founder of the Josephite Order, Mary MacKillop, also lived and taught here.

- Near Beachport you can relieve arthritis and rheumatism by floating in a salt lake seven times heavier than the sea.

- The Jimmy Watson Trophy for Australia's best one-year-old red wine has been won more times since 1977 by Coonawarra wineries than any other region.

- The Bordertown Wildlife Park is famous for its white kangaroos.

- The Riddoch Art Gallery in Mount Gambier is regarded as South Australia's finest regional gallery. It features national touring exhibitions and an Aboriginal art collection.

- The Woakwine Cutting on the Coast Ports Highway is Australia's biggest one-man engineering feat. You can view this marvel from a platform built for visitors.

visit to the area could be complete without investigating the rich and tragic maritime history of the 'Shipwreck Coast'. Following pioneer settlement and the growth of many towns, ports were established to serve the shipping trade. But the coast was lined with dangerous reefs and many ships went down, crew and all. You'll find their stories in one of the several museums that line the sea.

There are now four wine regions on the Limestone Coast, and they're among Australia's best. The Coonawarra with its red, red soil doesn't need much introduction, at least not to the world's wine lovers. The Padthaway area has been producing quality wine for over thirty years, while newcomer regions Wrattonbully and Mount Benson are making their impact on the industry. So after you've been to the Coonawarra, keep going! And while you're at it, tuck into fresh seafood all along the coast. Try a crayfish from one of the fishing sheds at Robe. The Limestone Coast – delicious!

Top: Coonawarra vines

Bottom: On location at the Blue Lake

Photo by Andrew McEvoy

Want More Information?

SA Visitor and Travel Centre
1300 655 276

Limestone Coast Visitor Information
1800 087 087

Limestone Coast website
www.seol.net.au/tse

National Parks and Wildlife SA
(08) 8735 1111

RAA Touring (maps and guides)
(08) 8205 4540

SA Tourism Commission website
www.southaustralia.com

***Postcards* website**
www.postcards.sa.com.au

Coorong Nature Tours
with Keith Conlon

David Dadd guides visitors through the vast and delicate Coorong wilderness   Photo by Jeff Clayfield

David Dadd is passionate about his own back yard. David guides interstate and international bird-watchers – and any keen visitors – on his Nature Tours through the vast and delicate Coorong wilderness.

He took me around Easter time, just in time to bid farewell to some amazing international ambassadors from their five-star summer house. Travelling annually to Siberia, red-necked stints are darting, busy little shoreline feeders about the size of a sparrow. They feed frantically to fatten themselves up for their epic yearly migration. After the northern hemisphere summer, they will return to the Coorong flats in September or October.

At Easter time, the Coorong sees plenty of people who come for a shack weekend, a lot of fishing and a little eating. David Dadd gets his visitors to focus on the bird-life – which does a little fishing and a lot of eating.

With David's help you'll soon recognise the custom-made beaks and legs of dozens of waterbirds who share the lagoons. An eighteen-year stint on the Narrung ferry between Lake Alexandrina and Lake Albert gave David the time to turn a passion into an encyclopaedic knowledge of the local bird life. And his grasp of local history and science is distinction level too. At Parnka Point, the narrow, middle part of the Coorong, between its long lagoons, he shows guests some leftovers of human occu-pation: an old cockle truck, a collapsed jetty landing, and the site of an old hand-pulled ferry that led to a farm on the sand-dune side.

On a Coorong Nature Tour you'll see dozens of waterbirds who share the lagoons   Photo by Jeff Clayfield

When the water levels are down David takes visitors across the salt pan, over the dune peninsula and onto the wild, awesome Ninety-mile Beach. And as day fades he'll take you walking high on the sandhills for a final thought for the day. He does it because he's close to it all – physically and spiritually. He wants us to take away a sense of understanding and caring. The Coorong is a wild, fragile place that needs our support and respect.

Contact David Dadd
c/– Post Office, Narrung
South Australia 5259
Tel (08) 8574 0037
or 0428 714 793
website www.lm.net.au/~coorongnat/
Day tour bookings on demand –
minimum four people

Coorong
Nature Tours

Piccaninnie Ponds

with Ron Kandelaars

From its boardwalk entrance, Piccaninnie Ponds looks like any other wetland on the Limestone Coast. But as the *Postcards* team discovered when we went snorkelling with professional diver Phil Argy, beneath the still surface you can explore a magical world of surreal beauty.

The initial experience of snorkelling is difficult, because the underwater view at Piccaninnie Ponds takes your breath away. You find yourself in a world where it's difficult to tell up from down. The water is translucent blue, and reeds sway around you and, fixed in the back of your mind, is the eerie knowledge that further down into the sinkhole there is a deep, dark labyrinth, where experienced divers seek out volcanic rock formations and spectacular caverns.

Phil Argy tells us that Piccaninnie Ponds was discovered by a couple of local divers in the 1960s. Once word got out that it was a fantastic site, divers came from all over the world to experience it, and you can see why.

At Piccaninnie Ponds you can explore a magical world of surreal beauty

Divers experience a full range of emotions when they venture down into the ponds – and fear is definitely one of them. And so it should be. While it's safe to snorkel here, people have died while scuba diving at Piccaninnie Ponds, prompting the establishment of rigorous guidelines about venturing into this underwater maze.

For Phil, cave diving is like an extremely addictive drug. While his descriptions of venturing down into the chasm and its world of caves seem like exciting adventures, he says it's a place that must be treated with infinite respect. Each dive, he says, is a humbling experience.

He'll always remember the day he pushed himself too far and suffered nitrogen narcosis, or what they call rapture of the deep. Trapped below a ledge, he was overcome by feelings of euphoria mixed with terror as he struggled to find his way to the light and safety.

At nearby Ewen Ponds the water is only ten metres deep, and perfect for snorkelling. The extraordinary beauty, an amazing array of marine life and the tide push you on through a series of connected ponds that eventually lead to the sea.

Whether you're a novice or experienced diver, the mysterious South East sinkholes will have you spinning. While experienced divers must obtain permission from National Parks and Wildlife SA to dive at Piccaninnie Ponds, you can snorkel without a permit both here and at Ewen Ponds. Earth Adventures and Blue Lake Diving both run regular Limestone Coast tours incorporating adventure caving and trips to the Piccaninnie and Ewen Ponds.

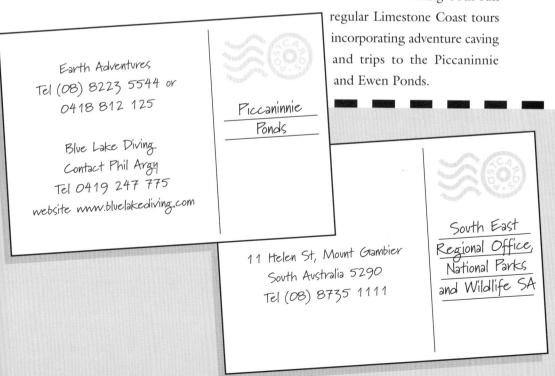

Earth Adventures
Tel (08) 8223 5544 or
0418 812 125

Blue Lake Diving
Contact Phil Argy
Tel 0419 247 775
website www.bluelakediving.com

Piccaninnie
Ponds

11 Helen St, Mount Gambier
South Australia 5290
Tel (08) 8735 1111

South East
Regional Office,
National Parks
and Wildlife SA

Highbank Wines and Honeysuckle Rise B&B
with Lisa McAskill

Bonnie and Dennis Vice travelled the world in search of the perfect vineyard location until they discovered a piece of high ground nestled on the ridge of terra rossa soil that defines the legendary Coonawarra wine region. Bonnie explains:

'Living in California we were exposed to wines from all over the world, so it was a wonderful opportunity when we were able to buy some small parcels here.'

The ridge of terra rossa – rich, red soil – is now covered with cabernet vines, but prior to European settlement the local Aboriginal people called this area Coonawarra because of its high ground covered in banksias or native honeysuckle. So, what better name than Honeysuckle Rise for the bed and breakfast accommodation nestled among the vines here?

Honeysuckle Rise was one of the first B&Bs in the area and was originally built from limestone rocks pulled from the paddock before the vines went in. Bonnie says:

'Like any dreams that are worthwhile, there's a lot of hard work but I think if you're happy with what you're doing, it's not really work. It's something that you like to do. That's the key.'

Wine lovers flock to the Coonawarra to savour the delights of this 'cigar-shaped strip of red dirt'. And for the novice, the vineyard views at Highbank Wines are just as heady.

This is an organic vineyard where, as Dennis explains, the grapes are hand-pruned during the winter months and hand-picked at vintage. He says that traditional methods and minimal handling help to ensure that every bunch of grapes delivers its full potential:

'The old-timers here in Australia did it that way and with our small operation it's an appropriate way to grow grapes sustainably. The Australian climate can ripen grapes far better than other acclaimed wine regions of the world and can also accumulate the acids that are necessary for the wines to live long lives. That's particularly important for people who are cellaring wine. We strive to achieve a combination of really intense fruits and wonderful aromas.'

Whether you're here to sample the local product or just soak up the view, Honeysuckle Rise provides the perfect location from which to enjoy one of the great wine districts of the world. And in the morning, you can eat breakfast in the mezzanine bedroom and take in the vineyards in all their glory.

Riddoch Highway
(five kilometres north of Penola)
Contact Dennis and Bonnie Vice
Tel 1800 65 33 11

Highbank Wines
and
Honeysuckle
B&B

Glencoe Woolshed

with Lisa McAskill

Half-way between Mount Gambier and Millicent, the Glencoe Woolshed rests quietly in a paddock as an imposing reminder of the days when Australia rode on the sheep's back.

Ian Telford, a former gun shearer from Glenburnie near 'the Mount', has a family connection with the South East that goes back to 1850, to the early Scottish pioneers who opened up much of the country around here. On the day we visited Glencoe, eighty-year-old Ian straddled the old post and rail fence out the front of the woolshed and filled us in on a bit of history.

Glencoe Woolshed is an imposing reminder of the days when Australia rode on the sheep's back

Glencoe dates back to 1843, when Robert Leake and his brother Edward crossed the Glenelg River in Victoria in search of sheep-grazing country. Although Leake hadn't intended establishing his property this far into South Australia, his Scottish colleague John MacIntyre told him they should press on. Ian takes up the story:

'When John MacIntyre was asked how he knew that this country lay further ahead, he told Robert Leake of the dream he'd had as a wee child at Glencoe in Scotland, in which he saw a faraway country with clover flats surrounding a lake.'

The Glencoe Woolshed was never mechanised but Ian still recalls how mechanisation in other sheds changed the way that shearers worked forever:

'It was a time of story-telling. There wasn't much noise in the shearing shed with blade shearing, but a lot of the joking, singing, whistling soon stopped once the machines started. It put an end to all the story-telling ... oh yeah, and it seemed to be more like hard work than a picnic then.'

Although shearing has an aura of romance now, Ian remembers stories his father told him of shearers travelling the country looking for work, poor living conditions, the

Ian Telford learnt hand-blade shearing from his father in the Great Depression years

1890s depression and the events that led to the great shearers' strike. At times, it seems that the landowners rode on the shearers' backs. In the good times, the wool clip made pastoralists very rich.

At its peak, 33,000 sheep were shorn at Glencoe each season, in a shed made from hand-sawn blackwood beams cut to exact measurements, identified by roman numerals, and then meticulously assembled. It was designed by W.P. Gore, a well-known architect responsible for many of the homesteads in the area.

On our visit, Ian kindly agreed to give us a demonstration of shearing – but not with a machine, he shears the old way by hand. But, manual or mechanised, there's one important matter that always needs to be checked.

'Hello Dolly. Dolly was the cloned sheep wasn't she? You've got to have a look at the gender to see what you're going to run into. Yeah, you've got to be careful!'

Ian learnt hand-blade shearing from his father when he was fifteen, way back in the Great Depression years. He may have slowed down now, he says, but in his day he'd line up with thirty-six shearers and go hell-for-leather to the sound of shearing blades cutting through the air on a cold South East morning.

No Limestone Coast journey could be complete without visiting a shearing shed. To visit Glencoe, the dream of a Scottish lad, you can collect a key from the Glencoe General Store.

Main Road, Glencoe
(half-way between Millicent
and Mount Gambier)
South Australia 5291
Tel (08) 8739 4320
Collect a key from the Glencoe
General Store – open daily

Glencoe
Woolshed

Tantanoola Tiger Hotel
with Ron Kandelaars

What's a fearsome-looking beast doing in a display cabinet in a South East pub with a Tiger perched on the roof?

These days in the front bar of this pub, the local interest in dogs revolves around those you can bet on. But while the punters may tell a few tall tales about the fastest dog in the land, nothing can beat the true story of another mutt who stands ever so still and silent in the dining room.

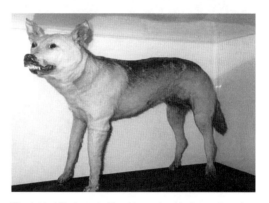

The fabled Tantanoola 'tiger' turned out to be an Assyrian wolf, believed to have survived a shipwreck off the coast

The yarn goes back to the 1880s, when South East shooters took off in search of a Bengal tiger believed to have escaped from a travelling circus. The animal was never found and the local papers continued to report sheep going missing as prey to a mysterious animal with feline characteristics. By 1893 reports surfaced of an unusual animal in the Tantanoola area. Some described it as the missing tiger while others said it was a very large dog. Reports became ever more sensational and before long, Tantanoola was a town besieged by a lurking beast.

Eager hunters scoured scrub country across the state's South East as the story spread and became more bizarre with each telling. Sightings of the vicious animal were reported from Robe, a hundred kilometres in one direction – to Bendigo, four hundred kilometres the other way. The hysteria travelled along the Glenelg River and to Donovan's Landing, the home of a true bushman, Tom Donovan, who went out in search of the fabled beast. He shot the animal that turned out to be an Assyrian or Russian wolf, believed to have survived a shipwreck off the coast.

Old Tom Donovan became a legend in the district. He toured the animal to

The Tantanoola Tiger Hotel

country fairs having no doubt urged the Mount Gambier taxidermist to stuff more aggression into his trophy. After all, this is a tale with teeth!

Despite the efforts of old Tom and his trusty Winchester, sheep kept disappearing for another fifteen years. Eventually a local chap, Charlie Edmondson, was arrested and charged with the theft of seventy-eight sheep. He pleaded guilty to the theft and asked for another four-thousand to be taken into account because he'd been stealing sheep for years.

Now Tom Donovan's wolf takes pride of place in the pub. Every so often the drinkers propose a toast to an amazing story – especially if they're celebrating a victory for the Tantanoola Tigers football team. Get along to the Tantanoola Tiger Hotel for some more tall tales but true. It's located on Railway Terrace at Tantanoola about thirty-five kilometres north-west of Mount Gambier.

Railway Terrace, Tantanoola
South Australia 5280
Tel (08) 8734 4066

Tantanoola
Tiger Hotel

Flinders Ranges and Outback

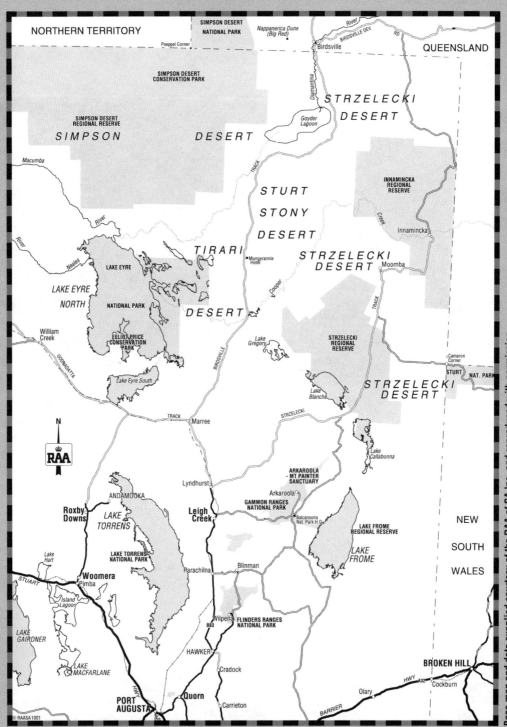

NORTHERN TERRITORY

SIMPSON DESERT
NATIONAL PARK

Nappanerica Dune
(Big Red)

BIRDSVILLE DEV. RD

Poeppel Corner

River

Birdsville

QUEENSLAND

SIMPSON DESERT
CONSERVATION PARK

*STRZELECKI
DESERT*

Diamantina

SIMPSON DESERT
REGIONAL RESERVE

SIMPSON

DESERT

Goyder
Lagoon

Macumba

STURT

STONY

INNAMINCKA
REGIONAL
RESERVE

River

River

Neales

River

LAKE EYRE

TIRARI

DESERT

Mungerannie
Hotel

Creek

Innamincka

LAKE EYRE
NORTH

NATIONAL PARK

DESERT

Cooper

*STRZELECKI
DESERT*

Moomba

William
Creek

OODNADATTA

ELLIOT PRICE
CONSERVATION
PARK

DESERT

Lake
Gregory

STRZELECKI
REGIONAL
RESERVE

Cameron
Corner

STURT NAT. PARK

BIRDSVILLE

Lake Eyre South

Lake
Blanche

*STRZELECKI
DESERT*

TRACK

Marree

STRZELECKI

N

RAA

Lake
Callabonna

Lyndhurst

ARKAROOLA
- MT PAINTER
SANCTUARY

Arkaroola

NEW

ANDAMOOKA

GAMMON RANGES
NATIONAL PARK

Balcanoona
Nat. Park H.Q.

Roxby
Downs

LAKE
TORRENS

Leigh
Creek

LAKE FROME
REGIONAL RESERVE

SOUTH

Lake
Hart

LAKE TORRENS
NATIONAL PARK

*LAKE
FROME*

WALES

STUART

Woomera
Pimba

Parachilna

Blinman

Island
Lagoon

LAKE
GAIRDNER

Wilpena
B83

FLINDERS RANGES
NATIONAL PARK

LAKE
MACFARLANE

HAWKER

BROKEN HILL

Cradock

HWY A32

Cockburn

HWY

PORT
AUGUSTA

Quorn

Carrieton

Olary

BARRIER

© RAASA1001

Base map and data supplied courtesy of the RAA of SA Inc. and reproduced with permission

Reverse: Balcanoona Creek   Photo by Bernd Stoecker

Outback South Australia is a land of stories.

Journey into a six-hundred-million-year-old landscape. Gorges, mountain ranges, sand dunes and salt lakes. A seemingly endless expanse, the Flinders Ranges and Outback is a diverse and vast region. You'll find thermal springs at Dalhousie, a bizarre mining moonscape at Coober Pedy, Aboriginal cave paintings, waterholes, and a barren desert world that can change with the click of a finger once the rains come.

Outback South Australia is also a land of stories, from Aboriginal Dreamings that have endured for forty-thousand years to fascinating pioneer tales of survival and hardship in a world where nature dominates. Legendary explorers Robert Burke and William Wills, John McDouall Stuart, Edward John Eyre and Charles Sturt all made their mark on this place. Today you can plan safer expeditions than theirs to this uncompromising terrain, by bus, four-wheel-drive or one of the many breathtaking scenic flight journeys available.

The Southern Flinders Ranges begins to rise just past Crystal Brook and from here it's a stone's throw to Mount Remarkable National Park near Melrose, the oldest town in the Flinders Ranges. The Heysen Trail winds its way through the Southern Flinders and is just one of the many walking trails in this unspoiled area.

Keith at Mount Remarkable summit
Photo by Jeff Clayfield

Tips From the Crew

- Ron recommends a visit to the beautifully restored Bruce Railway Station built in the late 1800s. It's now a hosted bed and breakfast.

- Keith recommends a stop-over for coffee (or bed and breakfast) at the rustic Bluey Blundstone's, a former blacksmith's shop at Melrose. It's the oldest town in the Flinders Ranges, and very pretty, with Mount Remarkable looming in the background.

- Jeff says you must see the Flinders Ranges from the air to get a real sense of its size and beauty. You can book with one of the many charter flight companies in the area.

- Trevor insists that careful planning is a must if you're driving in the Flinders Ranges and Outback. You can get a comprehensive safety brochure by calling 1300 655 276.

- Lisa says the best bait for catching 'yellow belly', or callop, in the Cooper Creek is shrimp or baby prawns.

The Australian Arid Lands Botanic Garden at Port Augusta displays a kaleidoscope of arid land plants and herbs. Here, there are walking tracks, a herbarium and a wonderful view out to the Flinders Ranges from the nearby lookout.

There's a terrific railway history to this region that encompasses great train journeys like those of the Ghan and the Transcontinental. Today you can ride the Pichi Richi Railway from Quorn, explore Peterborough's three-gauge system and model steam trains, or head further north along the old Ghan railway route.

Wilpena Pound is an awesome saw-toothed amphitheatre shaped by the Dreaming creators. In the central Flinders you'll find stunning Brachina Gorge Geological Trail and Parachilna's legendary Prairie Hotel. Arkaroola, a private wilderness sanctuary run by the Sprigg family, is unbelievably beautiful and now easily accessible by family car. Some of the tracks within, however, are real four-wheel-drive territory. The Gammon Ranges National Park is perfect for those who like a challenging bushwalk in rugged territory.

The barren spaces of the Outback lead to the famous Birdsville, Oodnadatta and Strzelecki tracks that travel through vast cattle properties. At the opal-mining town of Coober Pedy you'll find underground houses and shops, strange lunar-like landscapes created by opal mine mullock heaps and the Breakaways reserve, an extraordinary vista and favoured location for film productions.

Between Marree in the south and Marla in the north, about a six-hundred-kilometre stretch, you'll find Lake Eyre and the Oodnadatta Track that was once the railway line to Alice Springs. Outback travellers can follow the route of Charles Todd's Overland Telegraph Line and drop in to William Creek for a beer at one of the world's most isolated pubs. From there you can head by four-wheel-drive to Lake Eyre North. Just

 I Didn't Know That!

- Marree was once a staging post for camel trains carrying wool and supplies.

- You'll find memorials to explorers Burke and Wills along the creek near Innamincka, along with a marker showing where John King, the sole survivor of the tragic 1861 expedition, was found.

- Along the Birdsville Track are sections of the 5300-kilometre Dog Fence, built to keep dingoes out of sheep country.

- Visitors can peruse the night sky at the Arkaroola Astronomical Observatory which houses the largest privately owned telescope in Australia.

- The Port Germein jetty is a great place to fish and it's one of the longest jetties in the southern hemisphere.

- Oodnadatta took its name from the Aboriginal word *utnadata* meaning blossom of the mulga.

remember, check on conditions, let people know where you're headed and ensure your vehicle is equipped with emergency supplies of food, petrol and water.

The *Postcards* team has visited the Flinders Ranges and Outback on many occasions, and with each trip come new experiences and more waxing lyrical about characters they've met along the way. Pay a visit and gather your own stories of this ancient, vast and majestic region.

Lisa says the best bait for catching yellow-belly in the Cooper Creek is shrimp   Photo by Jeff Clayfield

Want More Information?

SA Visitor and Travel Centre
1300 655 276

Flinders Ranges/Outback Visitor Hotline
1800 633 060

Port Augusta, Flinders/Outback Visitor Centre
(08) 8641 0793

Free Outback Touring Guide
1800 620 373 or
www.theoutback.com.au

Road Conditions Hotline
1300 361 033

National Parks and Wildlife SA
(08) 8648 4244

RAA Touring (maps and guides)
(08) 8205 4540

SA Tourism Commission website
www.southaustralia.com

***Postcards* website**
www.postcards.sa.com.au

Pichi Richi Railway

with Ron Kandelaars

Travel through the Flinders Ranges after good seasonal rains, and you'll understand how nature fooled the early European settlers into believing that the Willochra Plain might one day become a great granary. And with the discovery of copper further north, the early optimism saw the construction of a railway line through the Pichi Richi Pass to Quorn. Well, successive droughts meant the dream of a railway across the Willochra Plain and through the very heart of the Flinders remained just that.

But the Pichi Richi line, one of Australia's most enchanting railways, continues to delight steam enthusiasts and holiday-makers alike.

Your journey starts at the Quorn classic bush station, across the road from the Transcontinental Hotel. Within minutes it's all aboard, and the W934 is rattling under a full head of steam. Soon the flats give way to a gentle rise on a small section of track, which for a time featured in two of Australia's great rail journeys: one heading north into the interior, the historic Ghan line, and the other from east to west, the Transcontinental, linking the eastern states to Perth.

You can only guess at the number of passengers who have listened intently to the slow gasp and heave of steam-driven beasts like the W934 as she hauls her way to The Summit. From the top, you can take in views of the Flinders Ranges as the line falls away, and then follow the road to Port Augusta before the train makes its way to Woolshed Flat. The early trains picked up their loads of wool and grain here, but ironically the railway was actually completed too late. By the time the tracks had reached the Willochra Plain, most of the cereal farmers there had failed, and it ended up being a railway to almost nowhere.

For a short twenty-year period from 1917 to 1937, many a passenger would have stopped along this network of steel as they made their way across the country. So the railway going nowhere became the centrepiece of a line going everywhere, and was particularly useful during the Second World War. As you inch your way across the bridge at Woolshed Flat, spare a thought for the thousands of diggers who crossed here on the way to the Pacific during the war.

For steam-train enthusiast Richard Atkinson, the connections with the Ghan which opened for service in the late 1870s and the Transcontinental, which began in 1917, make this a classic trip back in time, powered by technology that goes back even further, to steam:

'There's all that noise. There's panting from the Westinghouse pumps that provide the air for the brakes on the train, and you hear the steam sizzling out, and you can see it, and as you're going along it talks to you'.

A journey on the Pichi Richi railway starts at the Quorn classic bush station

Nowhere are the whispers louder than near the old Pichi Richi siding, where Richard and driver Chris Carpenter give this fire-breathing beast a few more shovel-loads of coal before opening her up for the trip back to Quorn. For passengers and crew, it's time to sit back and enjoy the views.

The Pichi Richi Explorer runs every Saturday from Easter to the end of October with additional trips during school holidays and long weekends. The Transcontinental Hotel offers reasonably priced accommodation and meals.

Pichi Richi Railway

Tel (08) 8223 7788
Bookings through Venue-Tix

15 Railway Terrace, Quorn
South Australia 5433
Tel (08) 8648 6076
or 1800 111 227

Transcontinental Hotel Bed and Breakfast

Arkaba Station Four-Wheel-Drive
with Lisa McAskill

Out here, the vastness of the Flinders Ranges can make you feel pretty small. Arkaba Station is home to Dean Rasheed, a name that's well-known in these parts. His brother Keith runs the Wilpena Pound Resort just thirty kilometres up the road.

Dean took over Arkaba Station in 1984 and immediately began grading an extensive network of roads. While the initial aim of the tracks was to help eradicate rabbits and feral goats, Dean quickly realised they could be used for tours of the property. Now this red-road highway features as one of the great four-wheel-drive journeys of the Flinders Ranges.

The red-road highway at Arkaba Station is one of the great four-wheel-drive journeys of the Flinders Ranges

Photo by Jeff Clayfield

As you begin to climb towards the spectacular Elder Range, glimpses of the unique pastoral history of this region come into view. Down below, the old wool-shed, dating back to 1856, acts as a reminder that Arkaba is still a sheep-station with about eight thousand merinos. Around August they're herded into a forty-stand shed for shearing.

Arkaba Station was established in 1849 after the legendary explorer John McDouall Stuart first surveyed this area. McDouall Stuart surveyed many properties including Arkaba, Aroona next-door, and Wilpena. No doubt his treks around the Flinders Ranges prepared him for his better-known epic journey from southern to northern Australia and back.

As you look towards the peaks of the rugged Elder Range and follow the tracks made by feral goats, it's not hard to imagine that there's still plenty to be discovered in these ancient ravines. Goat hunters recently discovered Aboriginal rock paintings in the ridges of the Elder Ranges, believed to be similar to those painted by the Adnyamathanha people at Arkaroo Rock, not far from Dean Rasheed's property. Dean says new discoveries abound on this property, including rare vegetation that occurs because of the area's higher rainfall. But it's not always easy. Most finds involve a difficult rock climb to get up to the caves.

Thanks to a permanent water supply in the nearby Arkaba Creek, this part of the Flinders has long been popular with the Adnyamathanha people and pastoralists. But in recent years the rock formations that snake their way across the landscape have lured a succession of geologists. Well over five-hundred-million years ago much of this area was the bed of an inland sea that may have stretched as far as Lake Eyre. Layers of sediment, built up over the ages, were eventually pushed skyward by incredible tectonic forces, creating what was once a massive mountain range. Now all that is left of the mountain range, believed to have had a similar mass to that of the Himalayas, are the quartzite sandstone formations that provide the contours of the Flinders Ranges we know today.

Geologists have found some fossils of ancient seabed creatures embedded deep in the rocks of these ranges. These creatures are believed to be some of the earliest forms of life that once existed on the planet. The find is so significant that it has caused scientists to rethink their notions of time.

So come and do some time travelling with Dean Rasheed in his four-wheel-drive. After a hard day's touring you can rest in cottage-style accommodation on Arkaba Station.

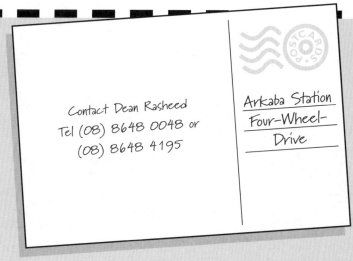

Contact Dean Rasheed
Tel (08) 8648 0048 or
(08) 8648 4195

Arkaba Station
Four-Wheel-
Drive

Pete Dobre, Photographer
with Ron Kandelaars

For Tess and Jed Dobre the great outdoors is an ever-changing classroom. Each year, along with their mum and dad, they scour the South Australian bush in search of the picture perfect. More often than not you'll find Pete, his wife, Cil, and the kids in a four-wheel-drive in the back of beyond.

When you're a photographer you expect the landscape to change and it certainly did on one of their many visits to Cooper Creek. Heavy rains transformed the desert into a carpet of flowers and shrubs, and the deep waters attracted hundreds of birds. Pete says it was exhilarating to walk on the flooded Cooper banks and imagine how it looked to Charles Sturt when he discovered this region for Europeans. And when the waters began to recede, the landscape and the bird-life changed yet again.

Each year the Dobre family scour the South Australian bush in search of the picture perfect   Photo by Pete Dobre

It's just one of the many adventures the Dobre family has enjoyed in bringing Pete's photographic record of our state to life. Their outback quest has taken them everywhere, including the thermal waters of Dalhousie Springs.

Their journeying was at first for private pleasure but Pete says:

'Friends used to come to our home and see our slide show – the dreaded slide show – and they'd say, You should do something with those images and share them with other people.'

Pete Dobre's done just that with his range of books, and in doing so he's also created a unique family environment so very different to his own unhappy childhood:

'If there's one thing that I'm going to do, it's to make sure my marriage doesn't reflect what I had as a child. I read to my kids every night and I tell them how much I love them because that's something that I didn't have.'

Throughout all of their travels, this family's ultimate purpose is clear:

'We see our role in terms of capturing God's creation, to freeze a moment in time. It's really satisfying to share that with other people. The beauty of taking a still picture is that it can never be repeated.'

Pete Dobre has published many photographic books and postcards depicting various regions in South Australia. You'll find them at good bookshops.

Tel (08) 8381 5895
Books available from
good bookshops

Pete Dobre,
Photographer

Grindell's Hut

with Ron Kandelaars

The rugged features, deep gorges and stunning hues of the Gammon Ranges National Park have long attracted adventurous travellers. It's a harsh environment but one that offers unspoilt beauty and a sense of true isolation.

For park ranger Christian Coulthard this is a special place. As an Adnyamathana man, he knows every nook and cranny of this National Park, and every gully and creek bend has a particular meaning:

'The Eastern side of Main Water Pound is the home for Akurra, the Dreamtime Serpent. Every now and then, on a clear day, you can hear his belly rumble and it sounds like thunder. One year it was very hot and dry and the Akurra came out of his home. He travelled through Main Water Creek looking for water and followed Arkaroola Creek all the way down to Lake Frome.'

A scenic flight over the Gammon Ranges instantly brings this story to life. From the air, you can trace Akurra's progress along Arkaroola Creek through the Gammon Ranges and out the eastern edge all the way to Lake Frome in the distance. According to Adnyamathana Serpent Dreaming, Akurra drank the lake dry and, with a bloated belly, made his way back again by gouging out the many ravines which slither their way through the Gammon Ranges. As he retreated to his home, Akurra left various water holes and springs along the way.

While the surrounding ridges are steeped in Adnyamathana stories, a tiny stone hut on the edge of a spectacular valley is pivotal to the pastoral history of the Gammons. At the turn of the century this place was about as remote as you could get. With high temperatures, basic amenities and an unforgiving landscape, it was a difficult place to stay sane. Out of this harshness came a white-fella tale of murder most foul, of sheep rustling and of two blokes who went mad in the rugged Gammon Ranges.

Opposite: A plaque on Grindell's stone hut tells a whitefella tale of murder most foul   Photo by Bernd Stoecker

A flight over the Gammon Ranges brings the story of Akurra the Dreamtime Serpent to life Photo by Pete Dobre

A plaque on the stone hut tells the story of John Grindell, a pastoralist who ran sheep in this valley back in 1918. Grindell fell out with family member George Snell, part-owner of neighbouring Yankanina Station. Each accused the other of rustling sheep and when it came to a face-to-face showdown, Grindell snapped and shot his son-in-law. He put Snell's body on a camel and wandered him around the bush for a few days in an attempt to fool the trackers. Eventually he shoved poor dead George inside a log jam and set it on fire. The police finally found Snell's remains and arrested Grindell in his remote stone hut. Grindell's death sentence was later commuted to life imprisonment and he was eventually released in 1928.

The early pastoralists finally gave up on their attempts to run sheep in this unforgiving country and the outstations are now run by National Parks and Wildlife SA. Visitors can stay in Grindell's Hut, Nudlamutana Hut or Balcanoona Shearers Quarters. All are available for hire at very reasonable rates. A scenic flight over this area is also highly recommended. Call the Visitor Hotline on 1800 633 060 for details.

Balcanoona Station
South Australia 5732
Tel (08) 8648 4829

Gammon Ranges
National Park

Warburton and Diamantina River Trip
with Lisa McAskill

Much of the interior of the South Australian bush is one enormous sump, where a myriad of creeks and rivers end their long journeys. Some of these, in big wet seasons, make it all the way to magnificent Lake Eyre. Lake Eyre North is fed by the rivers which have their source in the channel country in far away Queensland. After the heavy rains, the rivers and channels converge and are fed down to Goyder's Lagoon.

Our guide Rex Ellis says Goyder's Lagoon is like a giant kidney:

'It comes out the other side as the Warburton River. They call it a creek, which is an insult, I think. I call it the Warburton River and it's marvellous. I mean, there are hazards on it, but you get to know them.'

Whenever there's a big wet, enough to fill most of Lake Eyre, Rex sets out with a group to explore the Warburton, the Diamantina and Lake Eyre in a flat-bottomed 'tinny', an aluminium dinghy. Always close by is his old mate Stubbie, a Jack Russell dog with a love of adventure.

Out here it pays to come prepared with binoculars, camera and plenty of film; when the water meets the interior, bird lovers are in for a treat. The Warburton meanders pass coolabah trees and dense lignum, and it's hard to imagine that this waterway sits between two deserts, the Simpson and the Tirari.

In parts, the miniature red cliffs evoke memories of the Murray further south, and just as the swallows find nesting sites

There are many island hideaways to explore, along with the chance to see amazing bird-life

Photo by Pete Dobre

near the Murray, you'll also spot them on the banks of the Warburton. Rex's knowledge of the river is invaluable as it snakes its way to Lake Eyre. It's a route that he's taken many times before, including one in the 'big wet' of 1974, when Lake Eyre flooded:

'It varies every time you go down the river, but as you get near the lakes you sometimes get two to three thousand pelicans and all sorts of waterbirds, too numerous to mention. That's a real feature of the trips. It goes from a dead heart to a live, pumping one. But even then, with all that water in it, Lake Eyre can still have a desolate feel about it. I guess it's the lack of trees.'

You'll feel the isolation when you're out on this massive stretch of water, which seems to change colour with the changing moods of the day. While the lake is vast, it's not very deep, and a slight breeze can make for a bumpy ride. But there are many island hideaways to explore, along with the chance to see more amazing bird-life.

After the rains, you'll often find the normally barren landscape carpeted in wild-flowers. As Rex says:

'There's nowhere else in the world that you can do something like this, and South Australia's got it. It only happens every now and then but, when it does, we take advantage of it. And unashamedly too – it's just a marvellous trip.'

For a once-in-a-lifetime trip call Rex Ellis. He runs regular ten-day tours to the north of South Australia including boat rides down the Diamantina and Warburton Rivers to Lake Eyre.

Contact Rex Ellis
Tel (08) 8543 2280
website www.safarico.com.au

Warburton and
Diamantina
River Trip

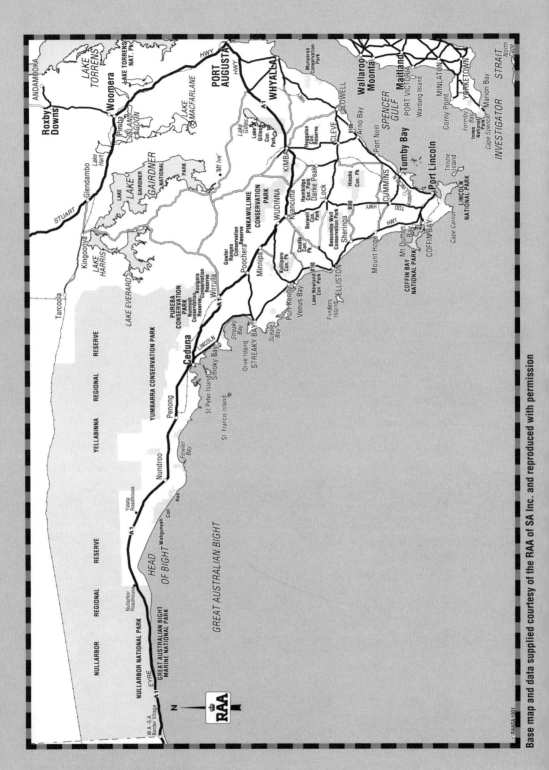

Reverse: Sealion at Baird Bay

Base map and data supplied courtesy of the RAA of SA Inc. and reproduced with permission

Stand on the Head of the Bight and watch the whales.

The northern gateway to Eyre Peninsula officially begins at the steel city of Whyalla. From this coastal hive of industry, you can embark on a spectacular two-thousand-kilometre journey along the coast to the border of Western Australia. You will marvel at towering limestone cliffs, drift along deserted beaches, stuff yourself silly on fresh seafood, trek and four-wheel-drive wild National Parks, swim with sealions and dolphins, fish from a beach, watch the whales, surf perfect breaks (or watch someone else do it), or just relax in a deckchair and watch the sun go down.

Gallipoli Beach, Eyre Peninsula   Photo by Jeff Clayfield

Of course, the Eyre Peninsula is not all coast. Inland you'll find rolling hills and a rich farming history. The 1500-million-year-old Gawler Ranges wilderness is alive with red and grey kangaroos and emus. You can spy on the one-hundred-and-forty bird species, including the majestic wedge-tailed eagle that glide through the sky there. And all over the peninsula, from late winter to early spring, you'll find blankets of wildflowers, including native orchids, boronia, correas and bottlebrush.

Port Lincoln, surrounded by stunning Boston Bay, was considered for the state's capital, but was eventually ruled out because of a lack of fresh water. The town has become a major grains port, the tuna farming capital of Australia and a popular seaside holiday destination. Boston Island sits out in the bay providing sheltered water for fishing and boating.

At breathtaking Coffin Bay, you'll discover great expanses of bays and inlets, perfect for sailing, swimming and diving. The area is renowned for its oyster production and

Coffin Bay National Park   Photo by Bernd Stoecker

excellent fishing. You can camp in the rugged, unspoilt national park there and take in views of the pounding Southern Ocean. Nearby you'll find one deserted beach after another and you can visit 'Anzac Cove' where Gallipoli was filmed. If you're still hesitant about setting off for Coffin Bay, just ask any of the fifteen-hundred or so visitors who expand the town to four times its usual population every summer. They'll let you know what a spectacular destination it is.

Lobster, whiting, abalone and shark, snapper, scallops, blue swimmer crabs and salmon.

At Baird Bay, hop aboard an eco-tour and swim with dolphins and seals. The waters around the old wheat and wool town of Streaky Bay are brimming with lobster, whiting, abalone and shark. It's also the place for snapper, scallops, blue swimmer crabs and salmon. In Streaky Bay's National Trust museum, you can explore the pioneering and farming history of the Eyre Peninsula. For a bird's-eye view, jump aboard a scenic flight that traces the nearby coastline.

In 1803 French navigator Louis-Claude de Saulses de Freycinet, who sailed

Tips From the Crew

- Keith says the Winter Hill Lookout, five kilometres out of Port Lincoln, has an unforgettable panoramic view. It takes in Port Lincoln, Lincoln Cove, Boston Bay, Lincoln National Park and the islands off the coast.

- Ron enjoys sitting on a jetty anywhere along Eyre Peninsula and dropping a line in as the sun goes down.

- Jeff, who should know, reckons Smoky Bay oysters are the greatest in the world. He also says the Axel Stenross Museum in Port Lincoln is a boat-shed-lover's dream come true.

- Trevor recommends taking an ATV (all-terrain-four-wheeled-motorbike) tour for spectacular views of Whaler's Way at Port Lincoln.

- Lisa says take off for a scenic flight along the massive Bunda cliffs to see dozens of southern right whales and their new calves during the winter whale season at Head of the Bight. You can book at the Nullarbor Roadhouse.

Murphy's Haystacks, Eyre Peninsula

alongside French explorer Nicholas Baudin, gave the name 'Murat Bay' to the area we now know as Ceduna. Although the bay has kept its name, the town was surveyed in 1896 and given its present name which was derived from an Aboriginal word meaning resting place. Blue skies, sunshine, mild winters and plump oysters from nearby leases make Ceduna a sumptuous repast.

Further on, at the legendary Cactus Beach, you'll find experienced surfers from all over the world trying their hand at three perfect breaks, 'Castles', 'Cactus' and 'Caves'. In nearby Penong you can visit a surfboard factory or book a camel trek along the dunes.

The Yalata Roadhouse is part of the 458,000 hectare Yalata Aboriginal Lands. There are about four-hundred people in the Yalata Community, many of whom commute from other lands in the north and west. The Eyre Highway travels through these lands but remember that permits are required for detours. Once you've got

 **I Didn't Know That!**

- Huge, pink and grey, wind-worn granite boulders can be found in several places around the Eyre Peninsula. One group, nicknamed 'Murphy's Haystacks', are believed to be 1500 million years old.

- The only mainland breeding colony of Australian sealions can be found at Point Labatt Conservation Park south of Streaky Bay.

- Cowell jade comes from the oldest and most abundant deposit in the world. It is believed to have been formed around 1700 million years ago.

- Dutch explorer Peter Nuyts reached the Streaky Bay area in 1627 in his ship the *Gulden Zeepard*.

- The giant cliffs along the Great Australian Bight are crumbly and have been known to break away. Whale watchers should tread carefully at lookout sites.

On location at the Head of the Bight   Photo by Jeff Clayfield

permits and visitor information from the roadhouse, you can try some excellent fishing spots or journey to the cliffs and sand dunes at the Head of the Bight for one of the world's best places to view the southern right whale. The time to spot them is during their annual breeding migration here between June and October.

Further west at Nullarbor, a labyrinth of caves and blowholes offer the chance to explore a bizarre and unique subterranean world. If you've made it this far, it would be a shame not to drive the extra one-hundred-and-eighty kilometres or so to the Western Australia–South Australia border, even if it's just to say you've done it!

Eyre Peninsula is a long way from the big smoke and so much of its coastline and hinterland has remained wild and picturesque. Plan to spend a week or two, and head on over. You'll love it too.

Want More Information?

SA Visitor and Travel Centre
1300 655 276

Eyre Peninsula Tourism Association
(08) 8682 4688

Eyre Peninsula website
www.epta.com.au

Port Lincoln Visitor Information Centre
(08) 8683 3544

Whyalla Visitor Information Centre
(08) 8645 7900

Ceduna Visitor Information Centre
(08) 8625 2780

Primary Industries SA Fisheries – Streaky Bay
(08) 8626 1247

National Parks and Wildlife SA
(08) 8688 3111

RAA Touring (maps and guides)
(08) 8205 4540

SA Tourism Commission website
www.southaustralia.com

Postcards website
www.postcards.sa.com.au

Whyalla Maritime Museum
with Ron Kandelaars

The people of Whyalla are rightly proud of their shipbuilding past, so much so that they have gone to extraordinary lengths to preserve it. Back in the mid eighties, the Whyalla Jubilee 150 Committee bought back nearly seven-hundred tonnes of maritime history, the HMAS *Whyalla*. After years of service as a navy corvette and later as a lighthouse tender, the *Whyalla* steamed back into town. She was then hauled two kilometres inland in a community project that gives new meaning to the term 'dry dock'.

HMAS *Whyalla* was the first ship built at the BHP shipyards in Whyalla in 1941, the start of a massive building program that saw sixty-six ships in all built there. During the Second World War, she was a Bathurst Class Corvette engaged in coastal surveillance of Papua New Guinea and convoying Australian and allied merchant men to the Pacific. The BHP ship-building program, which began as part of the war effort, continued right through to the late seventies.

HMAS *Whyalla* was the first ship built at the BHP shipyards in Whyalla in 1941

Seen in quiet dry-dock several kilometres from where she was built, it's hard to imagine that she was once attacked by Japanese zeros. And old skippers would certainly be surprised, to say the least, at the garden view from the bridge today.

As you wander around the decks, you get a sense of how crowded life would have been on board a wartime corvette sailing through the humid waters of the tropics. The ship was designed for a crew of eighty-seven people – and while the captain's quarters were by no means spacious, spare a thought for the rest of the crew.

Displays in the Tanderra Museum point to a camaraderie forged under the stresses of war

At any one time, up to forty men would bunk in a crammed space with many of the hatches open, so there was no privacy whatsoever. But the faded photos in the nearby Tanderra museum building point to a camaraderie forged under the stresses of war. The *Whyalla* often worked in heavily mined waters, much closer than many Australians realised. At one time, there were roughly seventy mines in the waters between Sydney and Spencer Gulf.

HMAS *Whyalla* later worked in Port Phillip Bay in Victoria, where she was renamed the *RIP*. Now she rests in peace alongside the museum, where you'll find displays outlining how the BHP shipyards grew, producing massive carriers that transported our iron ore and steel to the rest of the world.

Lincoln Highway, Whyalla
South Australia 5600
Tel (08) 8645 8900
Open every day 10 am—4 pm,
except Good Friday
and Christmas Day

Whyalla
Maritime
Museum

Coffin Bay National Park
with Keith Conlon

offin Bay is postcard perfect. This idyllic fishing town and port, forty-five kilometres west of Port Lincoln, is tucked away in a series of bays and sheltered by a long peninsula of sand and limestone that stretches up into the Great Australian Bight.

I began my journey into Coffin Bay National Park at the Templetonia Lookout, not far in from the township. From the high and sandy vegetated hill, you get a sense of a very different kind of wilderness. Way out west from the lookout is Point Sir Isaac. The Nao people knew it as the place where their Dreaming warrior Pullyallana took to the sky to become the thunder and lightning man.

The town of Coffin Bay is in the distance too. Despite what the wags tell you, its name has nothing to do with pine boxes for expired colonials. Captain Matthew Flinders charted the coast here in 1802 in the *Investigator*, and he named it after a helpful naval commissioner who became Sir Isaac Coffin.

The first station owners here ran thousands of sheep in this semi-arid territory. Despite the assortment of sheep, Timor ponies, rabbits and foxes that abound here, you still feel that you're in a remote place. There are inner bays and coves to share with nature and a chance to spot a great variety of birds, kangaroos, emus, lizards and snakes. Now and again you'll spot dolphins along the coastal park. A four-wheel-drive track leads to walking trails and campsites in magnificent surrounds that only Coffin Bay can offer.

If you believe the old saying, 'It's not the destination but the journey that counts', then a twenty-kilometre drive along a jolting track into the Park peninsula will reward you with a great variety of terrain. The destination, the uniquely attractive Black Springs Beach, definitely counts as a memorable spot. This low headland's craggy limestone cliffs are topped with coastal mallee. On the sandy curving beach, ancient and gnarled melaleuca trees cling to limestone slabs that reach the waterline. Away in

Coffin Bay is postcard perfect

the distance to the north, unexpected peaks and ranges at the bottom of Eyre Peninsula provide a perspective beyond the blue of Port Douglas, the vast inner bay.

I'd read about a turn-of-the-century eccentric, Wallaby Sam, and wondered whether he camped here at Black Springs. He once wheeled a barrowful of low grade 'seaweed coal' from the ocean end of the area all the way to Port Lincoln.

Black Springs is a designated camping ground in the National Park, but it is a case of BYO everything! It is one of many favourite nooks for dedicated Friends of the Park, Barney and Sally Williams. They helped our short *Postcards* expedition with their intimate knowledge of this wilderness.

We saw Victorians and Territorians gathered for a fishing camp at the dewdrop-shaped inlet Little Yangie Bay, and there was an incongruous line of washing strung up at Black Springs. Near there, an osprey perched high in a mallee branch over the water. It flapped languorously as it launched skyward again and soared away over a beautiful cove. Barney recounted magical moments with the Park fauna. He has seen kangaroos wade into the seawater at Seven Mile Beach, and he told us they could smell the fresh water rising to the surface from soaks below the tide line.

The trip back was strictly walking pace over the pockmarked plates of limestone that regularly mar the trail. But the bump and grind over the outcrops is worth it, with long smooth sand paths in between. Closer to the beaches or sandhills though, the sand can become very soft and difficult to drive on, but the views of the curving inner coast through sheoaks and mallee are captivating. We also saw emus and grey kangaroos close to the track. A grotesquely twisted stand of old tea-trees gave way to a hugging tunnel of coastal mallee as we drove towards another panoramic bay.

There are two distinct sides to the Park. In the lee of the long peninsula, the terrain is all sheltered sands with soft cliffs capped with graceful mallee. Out on the

Southern Ocean side, however, the craggy, high limestone cliffs fend off the full force of the south-westerly gales. The coastal wattle here crouch to the ground. Captain Matthew Flinders called this defiant edge Point Avoid. Even on a quiet day the swell turned into a powerful surf below us. Around twenty protected islands mark out the beginning of the Great Australian Bight here. Price Island looms large out to the west and, seemingly close across a reef break is Golden Island, its name inspired by the glow of the dying sun on its limestone cliffs.

Sections of the Park are easily accessible in the family jalopy, and if you're into four-wheel-driving there are many more treats in store for you. Coffin Bay National Park is a regenerating wilderness with its own unique moods and seascapes. Take the time to experience it, and remembers the rangers' advice – take great memories but leave no trace.

A coastal view from Coffin Bay National Park

Photo by Bernd Stoecker

Port Lincoln Office,
National Parks and Wildlife SA
PO Box 22, Port Lincoln
South Australia 5606
Tel (08) 8688 3111

Coffin Bay
National Park

Mount Dutton Bay Woolshed
with Lisa McAskill

The historic Mount Dutton Bay Woolshed

As the swell rolls in at the bottom tip of Eyre Peninsula, it's easy to see why a surfer, or anyone for that matter, would fall in love with this idyllic stretch of South Australian coastline.

Craig Brown was smitten ten years ago, and he stayed. Now Craig and his wife, Jacqui, and their two children have their own little portion of paradise. Craig spotted the historic Mount Dutton Bay Woolshed near Coffin Bay while returning from one of his regular surfing trips up the coast. These days, the restoration and maintenance of this classic piece of South Australiana is a Brown family concern.

Built in 1875, the Mount Dutton Bay Woolshed was the coastal link with wool growers for more than a hundred kilometres further up the Peninsula. The ketches came in daily during shearing season to take the wool clips to markets in Adelaide. Over a hundred thousand fleeces were shorn here, baled, and sent out to the jetty.

Over the years Craig has collected artefacts, like native oyster dredges and cockle rakes, which reflect this building's unique link with land and sea. And like any ingenious cockie he's managed to restore elements of the property back to their primitive best. The ventilation system in what was once the main storage shed is a winnower operated by a barbecue spit motor!

Craig Brown is a carpet layer by trade, and he's adding layers of history to a building that was once in a sad state of disrepair. But what drives a family to an old woolshed? Craig says they love the peace and quiet – and they bought it for a song.

The Woolshed was built by pioneer pastoralist Price Maurice, whose lease stretched from Mount Dutton to Elliston. At its peak, twenty-thousand sheep were shorn here in a season, which kept the shearers, classers and shed hands mighty busy. They all bunked in the old shearer's quarters, now converted into bed and breakfast accommodation that sleeps a family of six. There's also backpacker accommodation at the rear of the wool-shed, while the main complex is open daily as a museum.

In the late 1800s, twenty-thousand sheep were shorn in the woolshed in a season

Mount Dutton Bay
Contact Craig or Jacqui
Tel (08) 8685 4031

Mount Dutton
Bay Woolshed,
Museum and
Accommodation

Streaky Bay Fishing and Olive Island
with Ron Kandelaars

Streaky Bay is one of South Australia's best-known fishing towns. You'll always meet a steady stream of hopefuls arriving in search of a haul of whiting or snapper.

From the balcony of the Streaky Bay Community Hotel Motel you get a great view of the town's imposing jetty, where locals and visitors have fished for generations. Across the road at the Shell Service Station and Tourism Centre, you'll catch a reminder of some of the bigger fish to be caught in these waters – a replica of a white pointer caught back in the days before sharks were protected.

Streaky Bay jetty, where locals and visitors have fished for generations   Photo by Jeff Clayfield

Trevor Gilmore has tried about every kind of fishing there is to be done in these waters. He had the first oyster lease in Streaky Bay, one of the original west coast abalone licences, and he's been a commercial fisherman for twenty years. Now he ventures out to the edge of the continental shelf in search of giant crabs.

Today, Trevor and his fishing mate Peter 'Meggsie' Giles, are taking us out to Olive Island, named after the ship's clerk on board the *Investigator* when Matthew Flinders charted this coast two centuries ago. Flinders probably would have given the island a wide berth, because it's really a thirty-metre rock surrounded by other submerged rocks and reefs.

As we approach Olive Island, a large male sealion keeps watch. Although the island is the perfect breeding-ground for the New Zealand fur seal, the massive sealions seem most at home here. Before long Trevor manages to find a way into one of their favourite secluded bays and, within minutes, he's in the water swimming around with these playful creatures. I wasn't as confident, keeping a tentative eye on the watchful bull, but later I couldn't resist this truly extraordinary experience, swimming with three doe-eyed sealions who rose out of the mist from nowhere. Just as quickly, they turn on a sixpence and are gone.

There are times, especially when a big male cruises by, that I remember that thing hanging in the Shell Roadhouse back at Streaky. After all, these delightful creatures are usually dinner for the sharks that inhabit these waters. But today the males seem more concerned about others muscling in on their harem as they bellow warnings to protect their patch.

From the balcony of the Community Hotel Motel you get a great view across Streaky Bay

As Trevor points out, to help protect such a marvellous marine environment, visitors should play it safe:

'If you want to come out here, it's best to come on a charter-boat. You must notify National Parks and Wildlife SA for permission, as we've done today. The coast-line around here can be dangerous. If you're not sure where you're going, you'll quickly come unstuck, so it pays to have local knowledge.'

It was hard to leave a spot like this, but on the way back we took in Cape Bauer, named after Ferdinand Bauer, an Austrian painter on board the *Investigator* with Flinders who sketched many of the plants and animals seen along this coast. Later, we enjoyed a spot of fishing just outside Streaky Bay, and with these experts you don't have to wait long for a bite.

So not a bad day really. A swim with sealions, unmatched coastal scenery and a feed of crabs and whiting. To enjoy it for yourself, contact the Streaky Bay Shell Roadhouse and Tourist Centre and they'll put you in touch with local charter operators.

Shell Roadhouse
and Tourist Centre,
Streaky Bay
South Australia 5680
Tel (08) 8626 1126

Streaky Bay
Fishing and
Olive Island

Koppio Smithy Museum
with Keith Conlon

The rolling hills of Koppio at the bottom end of Eyre Peninsula are part of a standard tourist drive for any visitor to nearby Port Lincoln. This is classic farming country, with good rainfall and undulating expanses of top grazing land.

Koppio country looks a picture now, but for pioneers Tom and Adeline Brennand, who built the blacksmith's shop here, opening up the country was strenuous work.

Tom Brennand came over from Lochiel in the state's Mid North in 1903, when the whole pastoral area was broken up into farm settlements. He established the Koppio blacksmith's shop at what was then a remote crossing, confident that the passing parade of horse and bullock teams would provide lucrative business. He was right, and soon the Brennands had built their own stone cottage, a lasting monument to their pioneering spirit.

Not that such spirit has always been given the appreciation it deserves. For many years the smithy and the cottage were left to rot. But now, thanks to the efforts of National Trust volunteers Norm Jericho and Betty Duns, the Koppio Smithy is the centrepiece of a remarkable museum that has grown and grown.

The Koppio Smithy is not so much a museum but a village that tells the story of the early days of the Eyre Peninsula. One feature is an 1890s pug-and-pine cottage that was left to crumble in a field near Cummins, about sixty kilometres away, until Norm and Betty got hold of it. The cottage was dismantled, loaded onto a truck and put back together again at the Museum.

The old country store that once stood in Liverpool Street in Port Lincoln has had many lives. It was once a tailor's shop, then the local butcher, and now it serves as an entrance way to the Koppio Smithy.

Norm and Betty have done what many country folk would love to do – they've brought the bank to the people. The old bank building in the Koppio Smithy was trucked in from nearby Ungarra. The wheat agent's shed played an important role in

the district, too. Wheat was brought in from local farmers and graded before being transported to the nearest shipping port. The shed was transported here from the railway siding in Cockaleechie, and the old school was trucked in from two kilometres east of the Museum.

There's an amazing display of farm machinery in the array of sheds – like a Bagshaw winnower that was used to separate wheat from chaff in the early 1900s. And if it sounds like Norm Jericho is an industrious bowerbird, consider the bloke who brought a General Stuart tank over to the west coast. It was purchased in Melbourne in an army disposal sale, driven from Melbourne to Port Lincoln, and used for scrub-clearing south of Port Lincoln in the late forties.

Norm explains that there weren't many big tractors around after the war, so often the farmers would use whatever they could get their hands on. The powerful scrub-clearing tank has now been put out to pasture at the Museum.

Nearby, you'll find a replica First World War tank, used in the movie *The Light Horsemen*. Norm found it in the sandhills of Coffin Bay and, you guessed it, trucked it into the Koppio Smithy Museum. In the Pioneer Women's Room, old washboards and mangles now rest quietly as a reminder of the labour-intensive washing days of years gone by.

For Norm and his mates, the shed, complete with stationary engines, is sheer bliss. And all of this is but a glimpse of what's on offer at the Koppio Smithy Museum.

Opposite: The Koppio blacksmith's shop, established in the early 1900s

(40 kilometres from Port Lincoln)
RSD 1951, Koppio,
via Port Lincoln
South Australia 5607
Tel (08) 8684 4243
Open Tuesday to Sunday
10 am—5 pm

Koppio Smithy
Museum

Wakefield Press and Channel Nine thank the following organisations and individuals for use of their photos in *Postcards: A few of our favourites*.

Port Adelaide Visitor Centre, City of Port Adelaide Enfield, p 4, 14; Greg Aldridge, p 5; Penfold's Magill Estate, p 7; South Australian Cricket Association, p 9; Bradman Collection, State Library of SA, p 12; SA Museum, p 20; Lavendula, p 35; Primary Industries and Resources SA,

p 37; Allusion Wines, p 43, 49; Yelki by the Sea, p 53; Goolwa Maritime Gallery, p 55; Cape Forbin Retreat, p 61, 64; Hog Bay Apiary, p 66; Farmhouse Cheeses, p 70; Kangaroo Island Olive Oil Company, p 71, 72; King's Fishing Charter, p 75, 76; Peter Herriman, p 82, 84; Burra Visitor Centre, p 89; Food Barossa, p 96, 108; Southern Yorke Oysters, p 113, 117; Primary Industries and Resources SA, p 119, 120; Royal House Hotel Motel, p 125, 126;

Banrock Station, p 130, 136; Mannum Visitor Information Centre, p 131; National Parks and Wildlife SA – Mount Gambier, p 146, 150; Limestone Coast Tourism, p 154; Tantanoola Tiger Hotel, p 157; Eyre Peninsula Tourism, p 175, 179, 181, 182, 184, 190, 192; Mount Dutton Bay Woolshed, p 186, 187.

Vineyard Blues, p 80, is from an original work by Murray Edwards and is protected by copyright from reproduction in any form.